CALIFORNIA HOUSING MARKETS IN THE 1980s

California Housing Markets in the 1980s: Demand Affordability, and Policies

Kenneth T. Rosen

*Professor, Graduate School of Business,
and Chairman, Center for Real Estate
and Urban Economics
University of California, Berkeley*

 Oelgeschlager, Gunn & Hain, Publishers, Inc.
Cambridge, Massachusetts

State of California
George Deukmejian, Governor
Kirk West, Secretary, Business, Transportation,
   and Housing Agency
Susan Golding, Deputy Secretary, Housing
James A. Edmonds, Jr., Real Estate Commissioner

Funded by a Grant from the Education and Research Fund of
the Department of Real Estate, State of California, under Contract No. 83-314, for the Purposes of Developing Coordinated
Procedure to Expedite the Development and Construction of
Various Types of Housing, Particularly Low-Cost Housing—
Including Methods of Preparation of Draft Legislation to Im-
plement the Proposed Procedures.

International Standard Book Number: 0-89946-185-9

Library of Congress Catalog Card Number: 84-2368

Printed in the U.S.A.

Library of Congress Cataloging in Publication Data

Rosen, Kenneth T.
   California housing markets in the 1980s.

1. Housing—California. 2. Real estate business—
California. I. Title.
HD7303C2R67 1983   338.4'769083'09794   84-2368
ISBN 0-89946-185-9

Contents

v

**Chapter 5 Housing Policies for California
in the 1980s**

Tables and Figures

Figures

Preface

This book was prepared for the Department of Real Estate, State of California, under Contract No. 83-314 for $45,000 entered into with FBMA, Inc. It was prepared by Kenneth T. Rosen with the assistance of Katie Canon.

The main motivation of this book is to carefully set out the "facts" concerning California's housing market in the 1980s, and then to derive some innovative solutions to the problems facing the market.

Prior to the publication of this book, the Rand Corporation prepared a similar report entitled *California's Housing: Adequacy, Availability, and Affordability*. The Rand report differs from this book in its basic assumptions, calculations and conclusions. We deal with many of the same issues and draw some comparisons with the Rand report, but this work is not intended as a direct response to the Rand work.

This book details the recent past and future of the California housing market. It summarizes demographic changes; it explains the supply, demand, and cost of housing; it sets forth definitions and measures of housing affordability; and finally it reviews the impacts and implications of housing policy.

A number of people supplied data and comments for this work. We would especially like to thank Joel Singer, Kathy Schwartz, Ward Connerly, Preston Butcher, Ted Dienstfrey, Jane Goldman, Carol Schatz, James Edmonds, and Susan Golding.

Finally, without the extraordinary effort of Katie Canon this book could not have been completed under the short deadlines we faced.

Introduction

California faces a substantial set of housing problems in the mid-1980s. First-time homebuyers and first entrants to the housing market will face a continuing affordability crisis, a function of the rise in house prices and interest rates in the 1970s. This first time homebuyer affordability problem is having a substantial effect on the California economy by limiting its ability to attract and keep technical and professional employees. High housing costs are putting coastal metropolitan California at a substantial disadvantage in the competition for national economic growth. A set of policies that could clearly reverse the relative rise in California housing costs would benefit both the economy and young California families.

Despite the relative cost of housing the state is likely to see strong demographic demand for housing for the remainder of the 1980s. Basic demand for housing units in California will be over 230,000 per year for the next decade. Nonetheless, the first three years of the decade have seen housing production far below this basic demand level, implying that California may face a quantitative housing shortage when effective demand recovers.

The rental housing market, which experienced little new construction in the late 1970s and early 1980s, already is in the midst of a shortage condition. Rental vacancy rates in coastal metropolitan California are below 3 percent, considered far below the level necessary to provide for efficient and normal mobility in the housing market. In the last five years this has created pressure for rising rents and the corresponding political response of the introduction of rent control regulations. In addition to the quantitative shortage due to a lack of new construction, over 30 percent of the population is paying more than 35 percent of its income for rental housing. Thus, the rental housing market faces both a shortage situation as well as an affordability crisis for certain low income households.

The solution to California's housing problems is clearly complicated but revolve around one key fact—a high level of new production is needed in both the rental and homeownership sectors if present and future supply-demand imbalances and the corresponding further rise in relative prices are to be avoided. This book begins by documenting the demographic demand for housing in the 1980s. It then, in sequence, examines the affordability of housing, the supply of housing, and the restructuring of the housing finance system. Finally, it presents an analysis of policies that may provide a solution to California's housing problems and considers the impact of these policies on the state's economy.

Chapter 1

The Demand for Housing Units*

DEMOGRAPHIC DEMAND FOR HOUSING

Population

Of all the factors influencing the nature and extent of housing demand, size, age distribution, and growth rate by age group of the population are the most crucial. For a ten-year projection of housing demand only a segment of the total population is especially relevant. Specifically, that part of the population that is now part of, or will enter, the home purchase or rental market as a separate household unit in the next decade—basically the population presently over age ten—is the focus of attention. This includes changes in age distribution due to the natural aging of the population and

*Portions of the text were taken from Kenneth T. Rosen, "The Demand for Housing Units in the 1980s" (Berkeley, Calif.: University of California, Center for Real Estate and Urban Economics), Working Paper No. 80-14.

changes in domestic and international migration to California.

This analysis of housing demand contrasts with the work of most economic demographers who focus on the fertility component of population change. This component is less relevant to housing analysts since the population that will demand housing in the next decade is already born. Thus, short-term birth rate changes will not alter the number of housing units demanded in the 1980s, although these changes may have some influence on the size and possibly the location of units as a result of changes in family size.

Since birth-rate variations will not greatly affect housing demand in 1980s, there is only one factor that can change the size of the "housing-relevant" population for the next decade, namely, a dramatic change in net migration to California. Migration to California is critically sensitive to economic conditions in California relative to the rest of the country and is sensitive to economic conditions in foreign countries of origin. Both legal and illegal in-migration from Mexico is of vital importance in this regard. The key economic determinants of the migration process will be discussed below.

Migration

In the past decade net migration to California, both internal and international, accounted for nearly half of the state's population growth. From 1970 to 1982 net migration to California totaled 2.1 million, while total population rose 4.5 million. As Table 1 shows, the yearly net migration totals have varied dramatically. In the late 1950s and the early 1960s net migration was over 400,000 per year. By 1972 net migration had dropped to only 38,000. In the late 1970s and early 1980s, however, net migration in California has again surged to the 200,000 to 250,000 range. This is in part due to the large increase in international migration (over 100,000 per year) during this period.

As compared to those in the rest of the nation,the prime determinants of migration are economic conditions. Three key factors determine migration: relative unemployment rate, relative income, and relative cost of living. It is the last factor that is

Table 1. Migration to California

	Net Migration Chase/RDA	Net Migration Rate[a]	Net Migration Dept. of Finance[b]	International Immigration
1960	—			61,325
1961	399,735	2.4		64,205
1962	348,538	2.0		72,675
1963	377,030	2.1		79,090
1964	262,455	1.4		67,407
1965	226,776	1.2		67,671
1966	93,402	0.5		73,073
1967	140,456	0.7		69,150
1968	47,120	0.2		72,371
1969	137,389	0.7		71,183
1970	119,247	0.6		74,268
1971	53,934	0.3		69,825
1972	38,086	0.2		80,121
1973	96,385	0.5	28,658	85,062
1974	117,002	0.6	38,930	86,861
1975	163,433	0.8	47,928	83,184
1976	189,508	0.9	71,607	88,700
1977	182,265	0.8	71,986	91,796
1978	225,028	1.0	54,675	133,089
1979	183,578	0.8	89,566	N/A
1980	270,161	1.1	52,889	N/A
1981	204,247	0.8	44,602	N/A
1982	258,627	1.1	49,369	N/A

Source: RDA/Chase Econometrics, Department of Finance

[a]Percent—Net Migration/Population

[b]Department of Finance data represents fiscal years and based on driver license address change reports. It thus excludes non-licensed driver population and so is only a proxy for trends rather than levels of net migration.

heavily influenced by the high cost of housing in California. The high relative cost of housing is a crucial factor that is slowing the growth of the California economy and population. The two equations below show both the critical relationship between migration and income adjusted for cost of living differentials—(real income) and the relationship between the cost of living differential and the housing price differential.

Net Migration Rate into California = 184.6 (18.73)   (1)

+ 26.65 (National unemployment rate/California
       (6.74) unemployment rate—both lagged one year)

−218.44 (National real income/California Real
    (20.68) Income—both lagged six months)

$\bar{R}^2$ = .88   D.W. = 1.7

Relative Cost of Living in California =   (2)

.956 + .053 (Cost of Housing in California/
(88.6)   (7.04) Cost of Housing in the U.S.)

$\bar{R}^2$ = .84   D.W. = 1.8

From these equations it is clear that 88 percent of the yearly variance in net migration rates to California can be explained by economic conditions relative to the rest of the country. Also 84 percent of the year-to-year variance in the relative cost of living in California can be explained by the variance in relative house prices. It is thus quite clear that demographic and economic growth in California are very dependent on the affordability of California housing.

The nexus between population growth and net migration can be seen clearly in Table 2. This table shows six alternative population projections that are contingent on different migration scenarios. They range from the Rand no-migration forecast, which produces a population in 1990 of 25,370,000, to a high-migration scenario, which produces a population of 28,380,000 in 1990. Our base scenario of 200,000 migrants per year produces a most likely population forecast—of 28 million people in 1990—almost identical to the State Department of Finance base population forecast for 1990. For the purposes of our housing demand forecasts we will utilize the base migration and population forecast scenario, realizing that a set of housing policies that reduces the relative cost of housing in California can increase economic growth in the state.

Age Distribution of the Population

In terms of the age distribution, the age profile of the housing-relevant population is known with a fair amount of precision for the next decade. The impact of the post-World War II baby boom on housing (and other) markets could have been generally anticipated by an analysis that included demographic factors. Table 2 shows the startling, but highly predictable, changes in the age distribution that occurred in the period 1970 to 1982. The table shows a sharp decline in population under the age of fourteen of nearly 380,000 people. In contrast, the population in the fifteen to thirty-four year old age group increased by nearly 2.5 million people, and the population over age fifty-five increased by over 1 million people.

This shifting age distribution was directly caused by the changes in the numbers of births two and three decades ago. Figure 1 illustrates the dramatic changes in the number of births in the past three decades. It shows that while there was an initial surge in births following World War II, there was also an important "second wave" of the baby boom in the mid-1950s, which peaked in the period from 1960 to 1964. The number of second-wave births was nearly 140,000 per year higher than in the 1947 to 1950 period. In the mid 1960s this second wave came to a halt with a "baby bust" that lasted through the mid-1970s. During this period the number of births was over 80,000 less per year than at the peak of the "baby boom." Since 1977 there has been a major upturn in births representing a "baby blip." In 1982 births in California reached record absolute levels.

The impact of the baby boom on the age distribution of the population can be looked at in three ways: net change in people in each age class without migration, net change in people in each age class with migration, and gross flows in the age distribution of the population. Table 3 provides the age distribution through the 1970s, while Table 4 compares, in more summary form, the decade of the 1980s with the 1970s. The population aged fifteen to twenty-four will show a decline of over 800,000 people over

Table 2.   Alternative Population Forecasts of California (Thousands)

	RDA/Chase Econometrics		Base Scenario		High Migration	
	1985	1990	1985	1990	1985	1990
Under 15	5,734	6,394	5,739	6,405	5,744	6,415
15-24	4,087	3,583	4,127	3,663	4,189	3,787
25-34	4,782	4,767	4,821	4,846	4,882	4,969
35-64	8,556	9,767	8,600	9,867	8,682	10,020
65 +	2,741	3,183	2,743	3,187	2,745	3,189
Total	25,900	27,694	26,030	27,968	26,242	28,380

	Rand No Migration		Rand Medium Migration	
	1985	1990	1985	1990
Under 15	5,336	5,445	5,568	5,979
15-24	3,908	3,433	4,282	3,995
25-34	4,558	4,432	4,880	5,221
35-64	8,146	9,030	8,240	9,319
65 +	2,668	3,030	2,726	3,142
Total	24,616	25,370	25,697	27,657

	State Dept. of Finance	
	1985	1990
Under 15	5,662	6,189
15-24	4,415	4,056
25-34	4,641	4,854
35-64	8,462	9,593
65 +	2,817	3,297
Total	25,997	27,989

Migration Assumptions:
RDA/Chase Econometrics + 167,000 migrants per year. Age distribution from RDA/Chase.
Base Scenario + 200,000 migrants per year. Age distribution/RDA.
High Migration + 250,000 migrants per year. Age distribution/RDA.
Rand No-Migration + 0 migrants per year. Age distribution/Rand.
Rand Medium-Migration + 215,000 migrants per year. Age distribution/Rand.
State Dept. of Finance + 167,000.

the decade of the 1980s. This compares with a growth of about 800,000 people in the 1970s. This clearly reflects the drop in births that occurred after 1964. The ramifications of this population decline will be felt most by firms and institutions specializing in providing goods and services to this age group, such as colleges

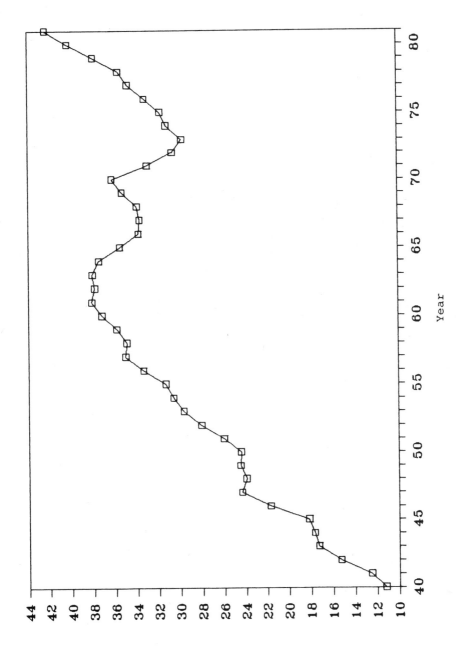

Figure 1. Age distribution shifts, California births, 1940-1980.

Table 3. Age Distribution of the California Population (Thousands)

Age	1982	1980	1970	Number 1970-1982	Change in Population Percent 1970-1982	Number 1970-1980	Percent 1970-1980
All ages	24576	23776	20044	4532	22.6	3732	18.6
Less than 5	1906	1722	1648	258	15.7	74	4.5
5 to 14	3420	3441	3890	—470	—12.1	—449	—11.5
15 to 24	4393	4491	3595	798	22.2	896	24.9
25 to 34	4535	4287	2698	1837	68.1	1589	58.9
35 to 64	7831	7402	6408	1423	22.2	994	15.5
65 and over	2538	2433	1805	733	40.6	628	34.8
Age	1982	1980	1972	1972-1982	1972-1982	1972-1980	1972-1980
All ages	24576	23776	20585	3991	19.4	3191	15.5
Less than 5	1906	1722	1634	272	16.6	88	5.4
5 to 14	3420	3441	3802	—382	—10.0	—361	—9.5
15 to 24	4393	4491	3770	623	16.5	721	19.1
25 to 34	4535	4287	2948	1587	53.8	1339	45.4
35 to 44	3152	2839	2338	814	34.8	501	21.4
45 to 54	2356	2356	2395	—39	—1.6	—39	—1.6
55 to 64	2277	2203	1794	483	26.9	409	22.8
65 and over	2538	2433	1904	734	38.6	529	27.8

Table 4. Age Distribution of Population for California: 1970-1990 (Thousands)

	Historical 1970	1980	Forecast 1985	1990	Population Change 1970 to 1980 Number	Percent	1980 to 1990 Number	Percent
0-14	5538	5163	5739	6405	—375	—7	1242	24
15-24	3595	4491	4127	3663	896	25	—828	—18
25-34	2698	4287	4821	4846	1589	59	559	13
35-64	6408	7402	8600	9867	994	16	2465	33
65+	1805	2433	2743	3187	628	35	754	31
Total	20044	23776	26030	27968	3732	19	4192	18

Source: U.S. Bureau of the Census, forecast derived from base scenario.

and universities. The impact on housing markets, especially the rental and mobile home markets, will also be substantial as these types of housing units are traditionally demanded by young households.

The growth rate in the population aged twenty-five to thirty-four also shows a dramatic change in the 1980s. This group which grew by nearly 1.6 million people in the 1970s, will add only 600,000 people in the 1980s, with virtually all of these people added by 1985. This group, will thus show a decisive slowdown in net growth in the 1980s, especially after 1985.

In the 1980s, however, the postwar baby boom bulge shows up most stunningly in the thirty-five to sixty-four year old age group. This group, which increased by only 1 million in the 1970s will add over 2.5 million people in the 1980s. While this group is still an important source of the stock demand for housing, most people in this group are already occupying a housing unit prior to entering this age group. While the younger portion of this group, aged thirty-four to forty-four may still be switching from owner to renter status following the life-cycle hypothesis, their contribution to incremental housing-unit (as contrasted with housing-space) demand is relatively small.

The final population age group that we have utilized, population over age sixty-five, continues to show a rapid growth and will add nearly 800,000 people in the 1980s. As a result, the proportion of people over age sixty-five will continue to rise substantially in the 1980s.

Combining the population age categories to obtain an overall population change profile provides some unexpected results. The growth in population aged fifteen or more will decline modestly in the 1980s. The population growth over age fifteen was nearly 4 million between 1970 and 1980 and will grow only three million between 1980 and 1990.

Nonetheless, if we exclude the population aged fifteen to twenty-four from our comparison, the numerical growth of adult population between the decades becomes comparable. It is clear, however, that the growth of the population under age thirty-five shows a sharp decline in the 1980s, especially in the second half of the 1980s. This measure of demographic change (net population movement by age class) is thus quite bullish for housing in the 1980s. We now turn to an examination of alternative measures of population flows that provides an even more positive interpretation for housing demand.

Gross Flows in Age Distribution of Population

In contrast to the net flow measure of population change, a gross flow measure of the age distribution of the population shows a somewhat later and more dramatic peaking in the high-potential home-demander group. Utilizing historical birth statistics and assuming very low mortality rates for the twenty-five to thirty-four year old group, we can calculate a gross flow of population by age. Table 5 shows these gross flow number for the 1970s and 1980s. It shows the largest number of people turning age twenty-five in the 1985 to 1986 period and the largest number of people turning age thirty in the 1985 to 1990 period. Over 0.5 million people per year will turn twenty-five or thirty in these time periods (versus about 400,000 people per year in the mid-1970s). Thus, the demand by first time households and homebuyers looks extremely strong. On the other hand, the number of people moving out of the twenty-five to thirty four-year-old group also rises dramatically in the 1980s. Thus, the gross movement into this group minus the gross movement out of the group declines dramatically in the 1980s and in fact turns negative by 1990. The net movement into this category was over 100,000 per year in the mid-1970s. It drops to 70,000 per year in the early 1980's and turns negative in 1990. Thus, in a gross inflow sense, with many first-time home buyers coming into the market, the housing market looks strong in the 1980s. On a net basis it looks somewhat less strong, especially in the late 1980s. In fact, housing demand does not depend on the age distribution of the population alone but rather on the interaction of age distribution effects with the household formation tendencies of households. A direct translation of the age distribution of the population into housing demand would be a mistake, for it is, of course, subject to a fairly wide range of uncertainty resulting from the forces that influence household

Table 5. Gross Flows of Population (Thousands)

	Age 25	Age 30	Age 35	Age 35-Age 25
1970	304	264	234	70
1971	296	265	231	65
1972	376	291	232	144
1973	380	327	243	137
1974	373	319	252	121
1975	392	319	270	122
1976	392	319	275	117
1977	405	393	295	110
1978	427	393	336	91
1979	419	379	333	86
1980	469	431	334	135
1981	484	440	335	149
1982	495	431	420	75
1983	505	466	430	75
1984	504	476	423	81
1985	518	494	446	72
1986	523	504	453	70
1987	503	500	442	61
1988	506	515	475	31
1989	503	509	483	20
1990	495	518	499	—4

Source: Derived from single-year age distribution—U.S. Census, 1970, 1980—and adding in cumulative estimates of single-year migration—1970-1990, Chase/RDA.

formation. We now turn to an analysis of the household formation process.

THE HOUSEHOLD FORMATION PROCESS

The demand for housing is determined by the manner in which the population divides up into households. A household is defined as a group of people occupying a housing unit. Households are classified by the relationship between household members and the household head. A family household refers to the head of a household and all other persons living in the same household who are related to the head by blood, marriage, or adoption. A primary individual household refers either to a household head living alone or one living with nonrelatives. Thus, the number and type of households depend not only on the age structure of the population but also on the way in which the population establishes or breaks family ties and groups itself into shelter-consuming units.

By definition, the growth in the number of households must equal the growth in the occupied stock of housing. Thus, a direct measure of the number of housing units demanded is the number of households. Household growth depends not only on the population growth and the age distribution of the population but also on the tastes and preferences of the population concerning marital status and living arrangements, on growth in real income, and on the price and availability of housing. In the past decade, the propensity of the population to group itself into households has undergone a major upward shift. Because of economic and sociological forces, large numbers of people have opted to form primary individual households when they previously would have been sub-members of family households. These primary individual households result from young individuals setting up their own household, (i.e.,by divorce), and from the preference of surviving elderly spouses to retain their own independent living quarters. This dramatic increase in primary individual households in each age group of the population has led to a large increase in the demand for housing units.

The formal accounting translation of the age distribution of the population into households is accomplished through a concept known as a "headship rate." The headship rate shows the ratio of the number of household heads in a particular age group to the population in that age group. The headship rate can also be calculated in terms of household type. The following equation sets out the precise translation formula:

$$HH_{ij} = hh_{ij} * POP_j$$

This equation states that households of type i and age group j (HH_{ij}) equals the headship rate for household type i and age group j (hh_{ij}) times the population in age group j. As stated previously, with POP$_j$ fairly well determined by our migration model and the natural aging process, the only major remaining source of uncertainty in the demand for housing units concerns the path of household headship rates and in particular whether the population forms family or individual households. A switch toward individual households greatly increases the household yield for each population group and thus increases the demand for housing.

Research done by the author and Dwight Jaffee indicates that three key factors determine secular trends in age-specific headship rates. The first factor is the level of real per capita income that provides the economic resources for the family or individual to maintain a housing unit. While there has been a rise in real income in the past decade, there has also been a substantial redistribution of income among household types. The sharp rise in the female labor participation rate is especially important in this regard as it has allowed female-headed households to maintain their own housing units. Also, the relative increase in social security benefits since the early 1970s has contributed to the ability of elderly persons to maintain individual household units.

These basic trends in real income have been complemented by a second factor, a sharp decline in the relative cost of operating a housing unit. The real price of a rental housing unit has fallen by nearly 15 percent over the past decade. This drop in the price of household formation has, in combination with rising real income, encouraged formation of primary individual households.

These two economic factors are further complemented by a third fundamental determinant of household formation, namely, a strong sociological trend toward individual fulfillment. The postponement of marriage by the maturing of individuals born during the postwar baby boom, the increased prevalence of social experimentation as reflected in POSSLQ (persons of opposite sex sharing the same living quarters) and PSSSLQ (persons of the same sex sharing the same living quarters) couples, and the surge in the divorce rate all work in the direction of increasing primary individual headship rates and increasing demand for housing units. This construct of headship rates as a function of economic and sociological factors is formalized in functional notation as follows:

$$\frac{hh_{ij}}{POP_j} = f(Y_{ij}, R/CPI, PDIV)$$

This equation states that headship rates based on age and household type are a function of real income, housing costs relative to the overall CPI, and the divorce rate as a proxy for sociological forces.

Household Formation Patterns in the 1960s and 1970s

This theoretical view of the household formation process is strongly supported by the available empirical evidence for California. Econometric evidence from the Jaffee-Rosen model supports this conceptual framework. A less formal examination of the data provides equally convincing support for this view. Table 6 shows the age-household type specific headship rates at five year intervals from 1960. These data show a dramatic rise in the proportion of individuals maintaining their own households. In the population under age thirty-five there has been more than a fourfold increase in the proportion of the population having separate households. In terms of actual numbers of households this effect is even more dramatic because these are the baby boom age groups. Somewhat less dramatic but still highly significant is the large increase in the proportion of people over age thirty-five in primary individual households.

By contrast, while the individual headship rate has soared, the family headship rate has remained largely unchanged (except for a fall in the twenty-five to thirty-four-year-old age group) in the same period. These two trends have resulted in a dramatic increase in the "household yield" for the population as a whole and is characterized by a reduction in family size as well as a reduction in the proportion of overall households who were classified as families. The young individual who moves out of her parents' home has increased the individual household headship rate without decreasing the family headship rate. A divorce in which

Table 6. Age-Specific Household Headship Rates—California

| | Primary Families | | | | Primary Individuals | | | |
	Under 24	25-34	35-64	65+	Under 24	25-34	35-64	65+
1960	.107	.409	.451	.336	.024	.050	.086	.258
1965	.106	.417	.457	.337	.029	.057	.088	.277
1970	.102	.415	.464	.327	.042	.079	.096	.303
1975	.103	.399	.452	.337	.067	.129	.107	.303
1980	.081	.339	.441	.308	.095	.189	.121	.301
1983E	.072	.324	.448	.319	.096	.206	.115	.306

Note: E = Estimated

children are present has the same effect, for the spouse with one or more of the children has remained a family household, while the spouse without children has become a primary individual household. It is crucial to note that these are not arbitrary definitions but actually represent an increase in the demand for separate housing units. This increase in the household headship rates is directly translated into an increase in the demand for housing units.

Table 7 illustrates the economic and sociological trends that have accompanied this sharp rise in primary individual household headship rates. Despite the decline in real income from 1980 to 1982, the fundamental trend in the California economy over the past two decades has been for rising real disposable income on a per capita basis. On a per household basis, real income has been flat, representing the rapid growth of less well to do individual and non traditional households.

During the same time period there has also been a remarkable drop in the relative cost of a rental housing unit. Since this is the main type of unit occupied by primary individual households, the causal relationship seems clear. Lower rental housing costs have encouraged household formations. In contrast, the cost of homeownership (using the CPI measure that is not adjusted for tax benefits or capital appreciation) has exceeded the overall inflation rate during this period. Since the relevant housing choice for most families is homeownership, the flat or declining headship rate trends of these groups are consistent with this price data.

Table 7. Economic and Sociological Factors Influencing Household Headship Rates in California

	Real Income per Person (1972 Dollars)	Real Income per Household (1972 Dollars)	Divorces/ Family Households	Rent/ Overall CPI	Female Labor Participation Rate
1960	3716	11,840	.012	1.22	37.7
1965	4119	13,174	.015	1.23	39.3
1970	4712	14,301	.022	1.21	43.3
1975	4964	13,888	.023	1.06	46.3
1980	5267	14,443	.023	1.04	51.6
1982^E	5174	13,883	.023	1.07	55.0

Source: Chase Econometrics/RDA, U.S. statistical abstract.
Note: E = Estimate.

In terms of sociological factors, the doubling of the divorce rate (see Table 7 and Chart 2) since 1960 is a major causal factor in the increase in individual household formations in the twenty-five to sixty-four-year-old age group. This dramatic surge in divorce rates must be viewed as fundamentally altering the nature of the housing consumer. Besides increasing the number of individual households, this high divorce rate has produced a household with a distinctive history of housing demand. A substantial number of divorced households have previously owned their own homes and have experienced both the investment and tax advantages of homeownership. As a result, a divorce is likely to produce a situation in which one spouse attempts to keep the house and the other spouse attempts to retain his ownership advantage by purchasing another unit.

The fundamental relationship between marital instability and housing demand can be further expanded to include several more speculative hypotheses. The rise in the female labor force participation can partly be attributed to the increased need of single, married, and divorced females to support or help support the housing unit. For a primary individual the relationship is clear—a job is a necessary condition to set up a household, unless one is receiving welfare or social security benefits. In the case of the traditional family household, the two-income household may be

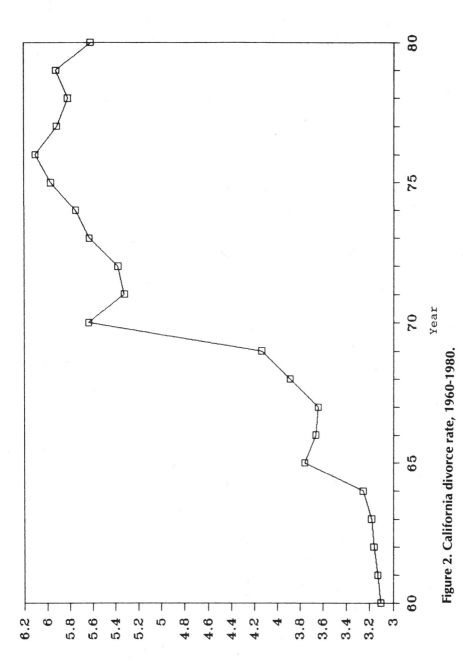

Figure 2. California divorce rate, 1960-1980.

essential to building up the downpayment and qualifying for the mortgage loan involved in homeownership. In this work environment the female may find a more appealing marital partner (of course the male may also find the new professional female more attractive than his present partner). In addition, this income provides the female with the financial ability to live alone. Thus, one could speculate that the two-income family necessary to support the house has also increased marital instability, which in turn has increased household formations and housing demand.

While the relationship between these sociological trends and the housing market are somewhat speculative, there can be little dispute concerning the fundamental restructuring of the California family into smaller and more numerous household units. Table 8 summarizes the distribution of households by type for recent years. These data confirm that there has indeed been a massive shift towards nontraditional kinds of households, like that implied by our headship rate chart. The traditional husband and wife family units have been the slowest growing type of household unit, showing only a 9.8 percent increase from 1970 to 1980. Husband and wife households now represent less than 54 percent of all households—down from 71 percent in 1960. On the other hand, nonfamily households showed an 88 percent increase during the same time period, and now represent one-third of all households up from 20 percent in 1960. In terms of absolute growth, nonfamily and single-parent households accounted for 923 thousand of the 1.312 million households formed in the 1970 and 1980 period. This restructuring of the California family has had a major effect on the aggregate level of housing demand (as shown earlier) and on demand in particular housing submarkets. We will now turn to the analysis of housing formation in the 1980s.

Household Formations Projections for the 1980s

The projection of household formations for the 1980s depends to a crucial extent on whether the dramatic increase in household

Table 8. Percentage Distribution of Household Taxes

Year	Primary Individual	Primary Families	Husband/Wife
1960	19.76	80.22	71.85
1961	20.03	79.95	71.09
1962	20.06	79.94	70.75
1963	19.27	80.75	71.00
1964	19.58	80.44	70.40
1965	20.71	79.27	68.91
1966	21.01	78.97	68.43
1967	20.89	79.13	69.24
1968	21.49	78.49	67.32
1969	22.46	77.53	66.75
1970	23.16	76.55	66.20
1971	23.40	76.13	65.12
1972	24.08	74.95	63.77
1973	24.81	73.77	62.72
1974	26.02	72.13	61.19
1975	26.65	71.06	59.87
1976	29.12	68.24	58.31
1977	29.82	67.13	57.04
1978	31.21	65.42	54.84
1979	31.74	64.52	—
1980	33.22	67.42	—
1981E	33.45	66.55	—
1982E	33.51	66.49	—
1983E	33.00	67.00	—

Source: Chase Econometrics/RDA.
Note: E = Estimate.

headship rates in the 1970s will continue into the 1980s.

Illustrative Trend Projections. To illustrate the critical inter-action of headship rates and the age distribution of the population, we will make three trend projection assumptions: (1) there will be a percentage point increase in headship rates comparable to the 1970s, (2) there will be no further increase in headship rates in the 1980s, and (3) the headship rate will increase in the 1980s at about one-half the rate of the 1970s. These illustrative calculations, which should bracket the range of likely possibilities in the 1980s, are shown in Table 9. Both headship rates and actual households are shown by age and type of household head. The sharp differ-

Table 9. Headship Rates—Household Projections: Alternate Trends

Household Type	Trend of the 1970s			No Trend	One-half Trend of 1970s
	1970	1980	1990	1990	1990
Primary Family					
15-24	.102	.081	.016	.081	.071
25-34	.415	.339	.300a	.339	.320
35-64	.464	.441	.418	.441	.430
65+	.327	.308	.287	.308	.298
Primary Individual					
15-24	.042	.095	.148	.095	.121
25-34	.079	.189	.299	.189	.244
35-64	.096	.121	.146	.121	.133
65+	.303	.301	.299	.301	.300
	Number of Households				
		1980	1990	1990	1990
Primary Family					
15-24		364	223	297	260
25-34		1453	1454	1643	1550
35-64		3263	4124	4351	4243
65+		749	915	982	950
Primary Individual					
15-24		427	542	348	443
25-34		810	1449	916	1182
35-64		896	1441	1194	1312
65+		733	953	959	956

aGiven the sharp decline in the 1970s, a somewhat lower trend would be indicated.

ences in net change in households depending on headship rate assumptions are shown in Table 10.

These tables show that if the headship rate trends of the 1970s were to continue, we would have a boom in the demographic demand for housing units over 250,000 units demanded per year. Individual households would provide nearly two-thirds of the incremental demand for housing. In contrast, if the headship rates of the 1970s prevailed, the incremental demand for housing would be only half as large, or 210,000 units per year. In this case, primary family households would account for over two-thirds of the incremental demand for housing. If we take a mid-point case,

Table 10.   Net Change in Households 1980s Alternative Trends (Thousands)

	Trends of 1970s	No Trend	One-half Trend of 1970s
Primary Families			
15-24	—41	—67	—104
25-34	1	190	97
35-64	861	1088	980
65 +	166	233	201
Total	987	1444	1174
Primary Individuals			
15-24	115	—79	16
25-34	639	106	372
35-64	545	298	416
65 +	220	226	223
Total	1519	551	1027
Total, All Households	2506	1995	2201

with headship rates rising at one-half of the trend of the 1970s, demographic demand for housing will be 230,000 units per year, with a roughly equal split between primary family and primary individual households.

Econometric Projections of Households-1980's.   An alternative methodology for forecasting household formation is to utilize an econometric model of household formation behavior. As set forth earlier in this section, the key variables influencing changes in household headship rates are: changes in real disposable income, changes in the cost of maintaining a separate housing unit (proxied by the rental component of the CPI), and changes in divorce and marriage rates. Separate equations were estimated for each age group and household type. As might be expected, primary-individual and young-household groups are most sensitive to economic variables. The sociological variables also have a large impact on young households.

In projecting household formations, the econometric technique provides a way of quantifying the impact of economic conditions that might differ in the forecast period from the historical period. In the 1980s we expect income growth to be lower, "real rents" to be higher, and the growth in divorce rates to be lower than in the 1970s. This last factor is especially important as we think that the divorceable pool of households is nearly exhausted. Thus, these changes should reduce household headship rate growth relative to the 1970s trend. While this is our base economic view, it is also possible that the economy could perform significantly better or worse than we expect. Using an econometric model, household formation projections can be made conditional on any set of economic assumptions.

Table 11 provides alternative household formation forecasts conditioned on these alternative economic scenarios. The econometric forecasts of household formation fall in a narrower range than our trend forecasts. They also show the sensitivity of household formations to economic conditions. The high and low economic scenarios show a difference of nearly one-third of a million household formations over the decade. Household formations range from 2 million in the low-growth economic scenario to 2.3 million in the higher-growth economic scenario. These numbers are quite similar to the one-half of the 1970s trend series. This is really not surprising, as the econometric technique has trends and cyclical effects built into the regression parameters.

SUMMARY OF THE DEMOGRAPHIC DEMAND FOR HOUSING IN THE 1980s

The demographic demand for housing in the 1980's, barring severe economic conditions, should be quite strong. Econometric projections and reasonable trend extrapolations show household growth, which can be translated directly into the demand for housing units, to be in the 200 to 230 thousand range in the 1980s. The growth in population and the changing age distribution of the population account for 150,000 of the household growth. This portion of housing demand is fairly certain. The remaining 50,000 to 80,000 annual growth in households is a result of household headship rate increases. These are in turn a function of economic conditions and sociological trends. In any case, the demographic demand for housing in the 1980s even in the pessimistic case, does look very strong.

**Table 11.   Econometric Projections of Household Formations
Conditional on Economic Conditions (Thousands)**

	1980	1990	Change (Per Year) 1980-1990
High Economic Growth			
Real Disposable Income	—	—	3%
Rental Component CPI—Overall CPI	—	—	1%
Households	8694	11,032	2338
Base Economic Growth			
Real Disposable Income	—	—	1%
Rental Component CPI—Overall CPI	—	—	0
Households	8694	10,870	2176
Low Economic Growth			
Real Disposable Income	—	—	—0.25%
Rental Component CPI—Overall CPI	—	—	—0.9%
Households	8694	10,702	2008

Source: RDA/Chase Econometrics.

REPLACEMENT DEMAND FOR HOUSING

In addition to the demand for housing units resulting from household growth, a substantial portion of housing demand results from the removal of housing units from the existing stock. The removal component of housing demand is far more difficult to measure than demographic demand. The major problem arises from the inability to obtain adequate data on changes in the quality and quantity of the housing stock. The major source of replacement demand arises from removals from the stock as a result of demolitions, fires, floods, and wind storms. In addition, conversion of residential units to nonresidential units as well as the merging of residential units can increase the net loss of housing stock. On the other hand, the conversion of nonresidential units to residential units, the subdividing of existing residential units and the rehabilitation of condemned units can decrease the replacement demand for housing by increasing and preserving the housing stock. While these types of conversion and alteration activity have been a major source of housing supply during certain periods of our history (e.g., the Great Depression period in the 1930s), they are extremely difficult to document. The only source of reliable housing stock data is the U.S. Bureau Census (1970 and 1980). Using these data and data on new construction over the decade, we can calculate a net loss of housing stock. As Table 12 shows the net loss to the California housing market in the 1970s was 150,000 units, or 15,000 units per year. Thus, the average net loss per year was 0.18 percent of the housing stock. The mobile home sector had the highest net loss rate, while multi family housing had the lowest net loss rate.

While the data and the theory about changes in the existing stock are not well developed, some generalizations can be made. Units lost to the stock because of demolition are related to three basic factors: government removal policies, the quality and age of the stock, and the level of new housing production. Government programs such as urban renewal, slum clearance, and urban highway programs all would raise the gross removal rate. On the other hand, urban homesteading and stock conservation programs would tend to reduce the removal rate. In the 1950s and 1960s the federal and state governments were involved in a number of removal type programs, and thus we experienced a fairly high removal rate. By the mid-1970s a number of these programs were being geared down, and a number of stock conservation programs were being instituted.

The second source of gross removals related to the quality and age of the existing stock. The greater the portion of low-quality old housing stock, the higher the removal rate. One of the dramatic developments of the last two decades is that the combination of government programs and private market actions has greatly improved the physical quality of California's housing stock. Table 13 shows that, by our estimates, there has been a drop of 120,000 in the number of physically inadequate (defined by inadequate plumbing) housing units. While the measures we have used do not take into account neighborhood conditions or physical defects (other than inadequate plumbing), they do indicate that the housing quality problem has been reduced. This is due in part to the elimination of nearly 300,000 units built prior to 1940 and the

Table 12. Sources of Housing Inventory in California 1970-1980 *(Units in thousands)*

	Single	Multi	Mobile	Total
All housing units 1970	4660	2162	208	7030
All housing units 1980	5724	3088	404	9194
Increase	1064	904	196	2164
Units added by new construction	1175	931	208	2314
Implicit net removals	−111	−27	−12	−150
Implicit annual net removal rate (%)	.00214	.00103	.00392	.00185

Source: RDA/Chase Econometrics and derived by author (includes year-round units).

Table 13. Quality of Housing Stock

	1970	1980
Lacking all plumbing facilities		
Number of units	143,676	21,756
More than 1.01 persons per room in units with all plumbing facilities (renter)		
Number of Households	551,163	638,610
Year structure built (000)		
1979 to March 1980	—	369
1975 to 1978	—	954
1970 to 1974	—	1,184
1960 to 1969	2,186	2,202
1950 to 1959	2,031	2,026
1940 to 1949	1,106	1,129
1939 or earlier	1,653	1,359

Year structure built—1980—percentage	Total[a]	Owner-Occupied	Renter-Occupied
1979 to March 1980	4.0	3.3	2.4
1975 to 1978	9.8	10.7	8.3
1970 to 1974	12.5	11.4	13.8
1960 to 1969	24.0	23.5	25.2
1950 to 1959	21.8	24.1	20.3
1940 to 1949	12.6	12.9	12.8
1939 or earlier	15.3	14.1	17.1

Source: U.S. Bureau of the Census.
[a]Vacant units included in total but not in owner and renter numbers.

addition of nearly 2.3 million new units. Table 13 also shows the age distribution of the the housing stock in 1970 and 1980. As a result of the policies and activities of prior decades, we have nearly exhausted our pool of low-quality, single-family housing stock. On the other hand, we have nearly 650,000 renter units that are over thirty years old and that may need extensive repair or replacement in the 1980s.

A final source of demolition involves the removal of units in order to allow the construction of new housing. During periods when there are high levels of new construction (especially multi-family construction), a higher number of older units are demolished to make room for this activity. In contrast, during periods exhibiting low levels of new construction this source of removal declines substantially.

The second major element in the replacement demand for housing is conversion and alteration of existing stock. This source of replacement demand involves the two-way movement of units between residential and non residential uses and the two-way movement between that portion of the stock temporarily not inhabitable due to condemnation, vandalism, or disaster. The net addition or loss to the housing stock from conversion and alteration is a function of public policy variables and overall market conditions. Public policy in a number of metropolitan areas has presently encouraged the conversion of non residential structures to residential uses. Similarly, market response to high levels of aggregate demand and the high price of suburban housing relative to older central-city housing have also made conversion and extensive rehabilitation more desirable. The combined effect of this conversion response is that by the late 1970s there were net additions to the housing stock from these sources. This contrasts to the early 1970s when conversion response led to net removals from the stock.

Taking into account all the factors discussed previously, it appears that the replacement demand for housing (in terms of net removal rate) will be somewhat lower in the 1980s than during the past decades. The low net replacement rates of the late 1970s will become the normal rate in the 1980s. As we stated earlier, public policy and market response has moved sharply in the direction of conservation and rehabilitation of the existing stock. In addition, by 1980 the number of occupied and physically inadequate units declined to slightly over 21,000 units—thus depleting the supply of removable stock. The only factors offsetting this downward pressure of net removal rates will be the aging of the multifamily stock and the expected high levels of new housing production in the 1980s, which encourage site assembly removals. Our best estimate is that the 1980s will see an average net removal rate of 0.15 percent, or about 15,000 units per year.

SUMMARY—DEMAND FORECASTS FOR THE 1980s

It is quite clear from our analysis that "effective housing demand" will be strong in the 1980s. The changing age distribution and the overall growth of the population will, assuming constant headship rates, produce a demand for 1.5 million housing units in California in the 1980s. Depending on economic conditions, increases in household headship rates can be expected to produce an additional demand for 500,000 to 800,000 housing units. In terms of "replacement demand," the most likely estimate (0.15 percent) indicates 150,000 units over the decade.

Thus, the demand for housing units in the 1980s will range from nearly 2.15 million to over 2.45 million units. The most likely estimates, based on our forecasts of economic conditions, show an effective demand for 2.3 million units. Thus, in contrast to the Rand report, the growth in housing demand will be at about the same level as in the 1970s. This represents an enormous demand for shelter in California in the 1980s.

Chapter 2

The Affordability of Housing in California*

In the past several years the popular press has declared an "affordability crisis" in housing in both California and around the nation. This crisis is said to have arisen because of skyrocketing housing prices and the dramatic rise in long-term mortgage interest rates. This combination has produced a popular press conception that only a small percentage of Californians can afford to purchase housing. It is often stated that less than 5 percent of Californians can afford to buy the median-priced home.

Contradicting this pessimistic view of the potential of homeownership are the statements, often in the same newspaper only pages apart, that housing is the best investment one can make and that more families and individuals are opting for homeownership than ever before. In this same vein, the Rand report states that Californians in general are not facing an affordability problem.

*Portions of the text were taken from Kenneth T. Rosen, "The Affordability of Housing in California" (Berkeley, Calif.: Center for Real Estate and Urban Economics, September 1981).

This dichotomous and seemingly contradictory view of the affordability problem with respect to owner-occupied housing is also prevalent in the rental market. Tenants complain about skyrocketing rents and demand rent regulations, while builders and investors cite inadequate returns to capital as the major source of the rental housing problem.

The purpose of this chapter is to carefully present the best available "hard numbers" concerning the affordability problem in California. It is only through the clear presentation of and agreement on the affordability "facts" that any solutions to the affordability problem can take place.

DEFINITION AND MEASURES OF AFFORDABILITY

As a starting point in an analysis of affordability, one must distinguish between categories of consumers and segments of the housing market. Five major categories of consumers must be considered: (1) first-time homebuyers; (2) first-time entrants to the "coastal metropolitan" housing market who were home owners in another area; (3) existing owners of "coastal metropolitan" property who move to another home; (4) existing home-owners who do not plan to move; and (5) renters. The focus of the affordability problem is clearly on the first entrant to the California housing market and on the first-time homebuyer in particular. A brief discussion of the affordability problem for the other categories of consumers is also provided.

Two basic measures of affordability for homeowners are usually examined. The most popular,and the one often used by financial institutions to qualify potential borrowers, is the ratio of current before-tax housing expenses to household income. Traditionally, an expense-income ratio of 25 percent was considered as the maximum affordability criteria. Increasingly, this traditional criteria is being modified to recognize the fact that nearly 80 percent of current housing costs represent deductible mortgage interest and property tax payments. Thus, for a household in the 30 percent tax bracket a 35 percent current expense-income ratio represents, after deducting tax benefits, no greater an expense burden than the traditional criteria. A household in the 50 percent income tax bracket could spend 40 to 50 percent of current income for housing and still be paying at only a 25 to 30 percent expense-income ratio after tax deductions. Given the very high level of nominal mortgage interest rates, it is incumbent on all participants in the housing market to adjust the old rules of thumb to an after-tax calculation. In order to avoid a cash flow problem, it is also important that households adjust their withholding tax to reflect their annual deductions of mortgage interest and property tax payments.

While an adjustment to traditional lending criteria to reflect the tax benefits of homeownership is essential, even this change will not adequately take into account the investment character of housing. Rapid price appreciation in California housing markets in the late 1970s has, perhaps incorrectly, made many households aware of the investment as well as the shelter component of housing. Thus, households may desire to spend more currently on housing, viewing part of this expense as an investment rather than a consumption expenditure. As a result, a more comprehensive measure of housing affordability would include all capital costs of homeownership. The *capital cost* of housing includes all current expenses minus current tax deductions plus the opportunity cost of equity invested in housing minus the expected capital gain from a change in the value of the house. Equations (1), (2), and (3) delineate the current before-tax, after-tax, and capital cost of housing, respectively.

Current cost of housing (1)

$$CC = [(1-\&) * P * i] + T * P$$

After-tax current cost of housing (2)

$$ACC = [(1-\&) * P * i + T * P] * (1-t) * Y$$

Capital Cost of Housing (3)

$$CCX = [(1-\&) * P * i + T * P] * (1-t) * Y + [\& * r - p^e]$$

where

& = down payment percent
P = house price
i = mortgage interest rate
T = depreciation and property tax rate
t = marginal tax rate
Y = proportion of current costs deductible
r = riskless capital market interest rate
p^e = expected capital gain on the house

It is the difference between the current and capital cost of housing that, in my view, has created the dichotomy between the "affordability crisis" and the "best investment" view of homeownership. The affordability crisis in California has *until 1980* been mainly a *cash flow problem* caused by the traditional level payment mortgage and the inability of households to continually monetize their expected or actual capital gains in housing. *Since 1980*, however, high real-interest rates combined with low house-price appreciation has created a *current and capital cost affordability crisis for first-time entrants* to the California market. We now turn to a more detailed analysis of the data.

FIRST-TIME HOMEBUYERS— CURRENT COSTS

First time homebuyers are frequently constrained by the current costs of housing. These costs, both before and after taxes, are shown in Table 1. The table shows that, before tax deductions, current housing costs for the median-priced house have risen from almost 25 percent of median income in California to over 57 percent of median income by 1980. The 1982 numbers are even more shocking—current costs before taxes were 62 percent of the median household's income. After-tax costs are lower because of the deductibility of interest and property tax expenses. Nonetheless, in 1982, after-tax costs for the median priced home rose to over 45 percent of median household income. By mid-1983, lower mortgage interest rates reduced this problem to some extent.

Table 1.   Current Costs—California

Year	Home-owner-ship CPI	Median Sales Price Existing Home	Effective Mort-gage Rate (Percent)	Annual Mortgage Payments (Dollars)	Property Tax and Main-tenance Costs (Dollars)	Down-Payment (Dollars)	Income (Dollars)	Payment to Income Ratios[a] Before-Tax Deduc-tions (Percent)	After-Tax Deduc-tions (Percent)
1970	135.44	$ 24,128	8.88	$ 1,732	$ 603	$ 6,146	$ 9,491	24.7	18.5
1971	139.10	26,324	7.81	1,779	658	5,934	9,605	25.4	19.2
1972	145.28	28,479	7.56	1,917	712	5,969	10,236	25.7	19.4
1973	151.54	31,574	8.03	2,170	789	7,218	10,853	27.3	17.5
1974	166.10	36,271	9.15	2,635	907	9,558	11,593	30.6	22.8
1975	192.48	41,100	9.20	3,085	1,028	9,962	12,437	33.1	24.7
1976	209.26	52,297	9.13	3,941	1,307	12,269	13,417	39.1	29.2
1977	226.58	63,713	9.25	4,845	1,593	15,023	14,359	44.8	33.4
1978	251.33	71,281	9.95	5,684	2,138	17,471	15,869	49.3	36.5
1979	275.23	82,680	11.08	7,035	1,658	22,157	17,756	48.9	35.4
1980	337.56	98,040	12.92	9,637	1,961	26,226	20,198	57.4	37.6
1981	386.98	106,040	14.72	11,802	2,121	29,002	21,867	63.7	44.1
1982	406.26	110,020	14.94	12,209	2,200	30,943	23,133	62.3	45.5
1983[E]	423.10	113,000	12.57	10,794	2,260	30,410	24,233	53.8	39.6
1984[E]	445.70	19,000	12.18	11,040	2,380	31,932	25,889	51.8	37.3

[a]Before tax payment to income ratio = (Annual mortgage payments + property taxes and maintenance costs)/income. After Tax Payment to Income Ratio = (Annual mortgage payments + property taxes and maintenance costs—tax benefits/income.

After-tax costs for the median-priced home, however were still near 40 percent of household income.

The sum of mortgage payments, maintenance costs, and property taxes must usually fall below a certain percentage of income in order to qualify for a loan. A rough rule of thumb used by many lenders is that current housing costs should not exceed 30 to 35 percent of income. Using this rule, if tax benefits are not taken into account, a California household with the median income has not been able to qualify for a mortgage on a median-priced existing home since 1976. If, however, tax benefits are considered, the median priced existing home could have been bought by a household with a median income until late 1979. Thus, high current cash flow costs, the major portion of which consists of mortgage payments, prevent first-time homebuyers from obtaining a mortgage.

Clearly this cash flow constraint is severe for many households.

Throughout the decade current housing costs (before taxes) in the United States as a whole were smaller relative to income than in California, as seen in Tables 1 and 2. Furthermore, California's before-tax costs rose at a faster rate and were by 1982 almost 25 percent higher relative to income than in the United States. For the first half of the 1970s, however, after-tax costs in the United States were comparable to those in California. There are two reasons for this apparent disparity. First, the calculation of tax benefits in both cases is not strictly comparable—the data on marginal tax rates and surplus standard deductions used in the calculations for the United States were not available for California. Second, interest rates and home prices were somewhat higher in California throughout the decade, and thus deductions were higher. While these factors were still evident in the second half of the decade, before-tax costs rose so much faster in California than in the rest of the nation that by 1982 after-tax housing costs were almost 6 percent more of the household income in California than in the United States. Still this difference is not as large as the difference in house prices, with California prices nearly 70 percent higher than the rest of the country.

Differences in house prices make it especially difficult for new residents of the California coastal metropolitan areas to purchase a home even if they owned one in another metropolitan area. Median house prices in the key California metropolitan areas were nearly all over $100,000 in 1983. This compares with a median house price of only $75,000 in California's Central Valley and with a United States median price of $70,000. These price numbers are reflected in a national median-price-to-median-income ratio of about 3 and a ratio of median-price-to-median-income of about 5 in California.

Another consequence of high home prices for first-time home-buyers, in addition to the cash flow problem, is the large increase in downpayments required to purchase a home. As Table 1 shows, the median downpayment on the median-priced home rose to over $30,000 by 1983. This is clearly a major affordability barrier for many first-time homebuyers. Even if the first-time buyer is lucky

Table 2. Current Costs—United States

Year	Home-ownership CPI	Median Sales Price Existing Home	Effective Mortgage Rate (Percent)	Annual Mortgage Payments (Dollars)	Down-Payment (Dollars)	Income (Dollars)	Payment to Income Ratios	
							Before-Tax Deductions (Percent)	After-Tax Deductions (Percent)
1970	128.5	$23,400	8.45	$1,514	$ 6,642	$ 8,734	23.9	22.2
1971	133.7	25,200	7.74	1,587	6,466	9,028	24.4	24.3
1972	140.1	27,600	7.60	1,744	6,440	9,697	24.9	24.9
1973	146.7	32,500	7.95	1,932	7,167	10,512	25.3	25.2
1974	163.2	35,900	8.92	2,235	8,815	11,197	27.1	26.6
1975	181.7	39,300	9.01	2,524	9,390	11,800	28.9	28.3
1976	191.7	38,100	8.99	2,734	9,982	12,686	29.1	28.4
1977	204.9	42,900	9.01	3,139	10,682	13,572	31.0	30.9
1978	227.2	48,700	9.54	3,732	12,126	15,064	32.9	30.7
1979	262.4	55,500	10.77	4,649	14,430	16,730	36.0	33.6
1980	314.0	62,500	12.65	5,926	16,670	18,747	39.9	35.6
1981	352.7	68,900	14.70	7,736	18,007	19,074	46.0	39.9
1982	376.8	69,280	15.12	7,843	19,069	19,970	45.4	39.5

Source: Derived by Author.

enough to qualify for a low downpayment, he still has to come up with over $10,000 in cash to purchase a first home in California. The characteristics of first-time homebuyers in California are shown in Table 3, column (1).

It is quite clear from these data that first-time homebuyers in California who can qualify for housing have an income far above California's median ($40,000 versus $25,000) and yet are buying a house below the statewide median. These statistics confirm the view that first-time homebuyers in California are facing an affordability crisis.

AFFORDABILITY GAP MEASURE— ANOTHER WAY OF MEASURING CASH FLOW PROBLEM

Another way of measuring the cash flow problem for new homebuyers is to calculate a measure of the gap between incomes

Table 3. Characteristics for 1983 First-time and Repeat Homebuyers of Resale Housing

	First-Time Buyers	*Repeat Buyers*
Proportion of all buyers	35.6%	64.4%
Median income	$40,000	$48,000
Median age	29 yrs.	39.6 yrs.
Household type:		
Single male head of household	15.5%	9.4%
Single female head of household	4.2%	7.5%
Married couple	66.2%	74.5%
Two unrelated individuals	8.5%	3.8%
Type of property purchased		
Single-family detached	86.3%	88.3%
Condominium	11.0%	9.9%
Median price	$94,125	$130,000
Medium-sized home	1,354 s.f.	1,702 s.f.
Median downpayment	$10,175	$26,700
Median loan-to-value ratio	90%	79.7%
Median debt ratio (PITI)	30.6%	27.3%
Median monthly payment (P&I)	$900	$936

Source: California Associationof Realtors.

and housing prices in California. Tables 4 and 5 show the income distribution and house price distribution in California in mid-1983. The affordability gap is derived by taking the annual house payments for the median priced house (subtracting the annual tax benefits and assuming a 30 percent marginal tax bracket) and calculating the income required to afford the house, assuming that only 30 percent of income is spent for housing. This required income is then compared with the income distribution to determine the percentage of the population that cannot afford to purchase the median priced house. As Table 6 shows, 37 percent of the population was priced out of the homeownership market in 1970. The affordability gap had risen to over 68 percent by 1982 due to rising house prices and mortgage rates. By mid 1983 the affordability gap had fallen along with interest rates to 60 percent. This still implies that 60 percent of the population cannot afford to buy the median-priced home. Since 55 percent already own

Table 4. Income Distribution of Households— California (1969, 1979, 1983)

	1983^E	1979	1969
(15,000	30.7%	40.9%	73.3%
15-19,999	10.2	13.3	} 20.6
20-24,999	9.8	12.1	
25-34,999	16.1	16.5	} 5.2
35-49,999	15.3	10.7	
50,000+	18.2	6.4	0.9

Note: E = Estimate.
Source: U.S. Bureau of the Census (1969, 1979), 1983—derived.

Table 5. Home Price Distribution—California (1983)

House Price Distribution—September 1983 (in thousands)	
Less than 60	6.7%
60-70	5.3
70-80	8.1
80-90	10.5
90-100	9.1
100-120	16.0
120-140	12.8
140-160	8.5
160-180	6.2
180-200	3.8
200-250	5.6
250 and over	7.2

Source: California Real Estate Trends Newsletter, California Association of Realtors.

their own home, it must be emphasized that the affordability gap measure applies to new entrants to the housing market.

While most attention focuses on the affordability of the median-priced house by the median income family, there is in fact a wide distribution of both incomes and house prices in California. Thus, the affordability crisis might be eased if an above-median-income family were to buy a below-median-priced house. Of course, many professional families (with three times the median income) often complain they cannot find a median-priced house. In essence, what they are saying is that they want a house higher than median quality, but they do not want to pay for it.

Table 6. Affordability Gap

	Annual Payments for Median-Priced House[a]	Income Needed to Afford Based on 30% of Income	Percentage of Californians Unable to Afford Median-Priced House
1970	1,611	5,370	37%
1971	1,654	5,513	37%
1972	1,775	5,917	37%
1973	2,016	6,720	38%
1974	2,455	8,183	42%
1975	2,848	9,493	45%
1976	3,630	12,100	53%
1977	4,459	14,863	59%
1978	5,459	18,197	59%
1979	6,460	21,533	58%
1980	7,867	26,223	64%
1981	9,741	32,470	68%
1982	10,140	33,800	67%
1983[E]	9,188	30,626	60%
1984[E]	9,962	33,207	60%

[a]Calculated as mortgage interest payments plus property tax plus maintenance—tax savings, assuming a 30 percent marginal tax bracket.

CAPITAL COST OF HOMEOWNERSHIP

An alternative and more inclusive measure of the cost of home ownership is the capital costs of housing. It includes mortgage interest payments, the opportunity cost of the equity invested in the home, and the costs of insurance, maintenance, repairs, and property taxes. In addition, homeowners receive the benefits of being able to deduct interest and property tax payments on their federal income tax. Homeowners (especially in the 1970s) can also expect the value of their home to appreciate. Thus, the capital cost of housing includes a measure of the change in the household's wealth due to house-price appreciation. The capital gains included in this calculation, while properly a component of wealth, are not realized until the house is sold. Thus, capital costs must be carefully distinguished from the cash flow costs that were measured in Table 1.

Table 7 outlines the capital costs and benefits of homeownership in California for the past fifteen years. The most striking aspect of this table is that the capital costs of homeownership were actually negative throughout most of the 1970s. The net gain homeowners experienced in the last half of the decade rose to nearly 15 to 20 percent of median household income. These gains have been declining since 1979, partially because of the rapid increase in mortgage interest rates and the deceleration of home prices since that period. By mid 1983 the the capital cost of owning a home became extremely high—over 33 percent. The California capital cost numbers indicate that the net gains experienced from homeownership have declined sharply in the last several years due to rising real mortgage interest costs and smaller expected capital gains. Homes can no longer be considered the great investment they were five years ago.

EXISTING HOMEOWNERS

Homeowners who do not plan to move do not face the same housing costs as those who plan to buy a home. Their costs are based on historical costs namely, the interest rate and home price that existed when they bought their homes. Those homeowners who plan to move, however, will face current home prices and interest rates if their home is not "creatively financed." In addition, the homeowner will face an approximate doubling of property taxes as the new buyer loses the protection of Proposition 13, which bases his property taxes on 1975 property valuation for houses not sold.

On the other hand, movers will also reap the benefits of rising home prices in the form of the capital gains they receive by selling their current house. These capital gains can either be used to make a larger down payment and reduce monthly payments or can be invested, and that interest income can be used to offset the mortgage payments on the newly purchased unit. In a cash flow sense, existing homeowners clearly face substantially higher

Table 7. Capital Costs of Homeownership in California

Year	Mortgage Interest	Opportunity[a] Cost of Equity	Maintenance plus Property Taxes	Tax Benefits[b]	Expected Capital Gains[c]	Total Capital Cost	Capital Cost/ Income
1970	$ 1,597	$ 546	$ 603	$ 589	$ 761	$ 1,396	15.98 %
1971	1,592	463	658	596	1,778	339	3.75
1972	1,702	451	712	639	1,793	433	4.46
1973	1,956	580	789	729	2,963	(367)	(3.38)
1974	2,444	876	907	896	4,102	(771)	(6.65)
1975	2,865	917	1,028	1,045	5,351	(1,586)	(12.75)
1976	3,655	1,120	1,307	1,332	6,908	(2,158)	(16.10)
1977	4,504	1,390	1,593	1,638	9,147	(3,298)	(22.90)
1978	5,354	1,738	2,138	2,033	10,060	(2,863)	(18.00)
1979	7,215	2,455	1,658	2,413	10,194	(1,279)	(5.80)
1980	9,278	3,388	1,961	3,372	11,442	(187)	(.90)
1981	11,340	4,269	2,121	3,720	11,586	2,424	11.10
1982	11,814	4,622	2,200	3,874	9,047	5,715	24.70
1983[E]	10,381	3,822	2,260	3,453	4,987	8,023	33.10
1984[E]	11,341	3,889	2,380	3,759	4,320	9,531	36.8

[a]Valued at the mortgage rate
[b]Valued at 30 percent marginal tax rate
[c]A three-year moving average of actual capital gains

costs due to current interest rates and property taxes. While this will be offset in part by the value of the homeowner's equity from his previous home (as it could be invested elsewhere and could be earning a return for the homeowner), in reality, the homeowner cannot effectively monetize his equity unless the homeowner moves to South Dakota or Indiana. Table 3, column (2), shows these characteristics for movers.

RENTAL AFFORDABILITY

The late 1970s have seen the spread of rental control and the general complaints by tenants that rents are rising too fast. In fact, just the opposite has been true. On the average, in California rents have risen less than the overall inflation rate and less than the income of renters. Rental costs during the seventies and early 1980s are outlined in Table 8 and Figure 1. Median rent rose at about a 7 percent annual rate during the

Table 8. Rental Costs in California

Year	Rental CPI	Median Rent[a]	Rent/All Household Income	Median Renter Income[b]	Rent/ Renter Income
1970	144.7	$1,534	16.2%	$ 6,787	22.6%
1971	151.2	1,601	16.7	6,938	23.1
1972	154.6	1,639	16.0	7,354	22.3
1973	159.1	1,686	15.5	7,850	21.5
1974	166.8	1,768	15.3	8,223	21.5
1975	175.2	1,857	14.9	8,627	21.5
1976	187.0	1,982	14.8	9,316	21.3
1977	202.9	2,151	15.0	10,157	21.2
1978	220.5	2,337	14.7	11,110	21.0
1979	242.5	2,570	14.5	12,363	20.8
1980	268.7	2,848	14.1	13,789	20.7
1981	298.5	3,163	14.5	—	—
1982	325.8	3,452	14.9	—	—
1983E	344.5	3,651	15.0	—	—
1984E	361.6	3,832	14.8	—	—

Note: E = Estimate.

[a]Median rent is calculated from the Annual Housing Survey (1970, 1974, and 1975) and the ratio of median rent to rental CPI ($10.5998) is multiplied by rental CPI to obtain values for remaining years.

[b]Median renter income is a weighted average of data from the Annual Housing Survey (1970, 1974, and 1975). Growth rates are applied to derive values for years for which there were no data.

decade, while the median renter income rose at about an 8 percent annual rate. Thus, rental costs were a declining portion of income for households, falling from 16.2 percent of income in 1970 to 14.1 percent of income in 1980. Since 1980 there has been a small rise in real rents reversing this favorable trend with rents rising to 15 percent of income in 1983. In general, the national figures for rental costs show the same trend as the California numbers. Throughout the decade rental costs nationwide were a slightly higher portion of income in the United States as a whole than in California.

It is quite clear from these numbers that in general there is no "rental affordability" problem. However, a closer cross tabulation of rental costs with income (Table 9) provided by the Rand study

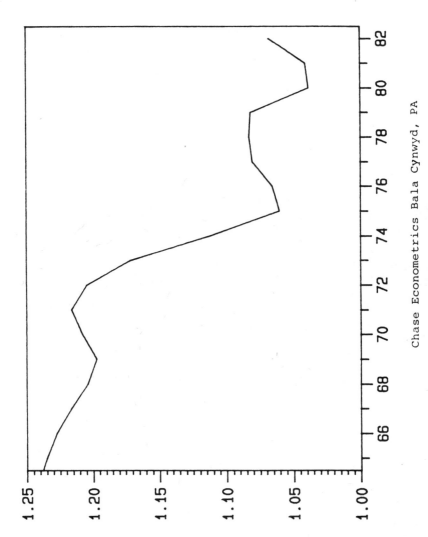

Chase Econometrics Bala Cynwyd, PA

Figure 1. California ratio of CPI rental component to total CPI, 1966-1982.

Table 9.   Rent Income Ratio (1980)—California Renters

| | Rent as a Percent of Income | | | | |
	Under 15%	15 to 24%	25 to 34%	35% +	Average Rent/Income
Income Class					
Very Low	0.9	8.4	11.1	79.6	60%
Low	4.7	22.2	35.0	38.1	33%
Moderate	14.4	49.9	24.1	11.6	23%
High	51.4	41.5	5.9	1.2	15%
All Households	14.5%	32.2%	21.0%	32.3%	33%

Source: "California Housing—Adequacy, Availability, and Affordability," Rand, October 1983.

indicates that one-third of the population faces a severe rental-income squeeze, spending over 35 percent of their income on housing. Equally serious from the viewpoint of the housing market is the failure of rents to keep pace with inflation and induce a supply of new construction. Public policy should thus attempt to accelerate rather than control rent increases to induce new supply and increase subsidies to those poor households who cannot afford even the modest rental costs in most locations.

CONCLUSION

By any measure, first-time entrants to the homeownership market in metropolitan California are facing an affordability crisis. High real-mortgage interest rates and low rates of house-price inflation make current and capital costs of ownership unaffordable for over 60 percent of California households. Even the majority of existing households could not afford to buy the house they now live in at current interest rates, prices, and property taxes.

In the rental housing sector, a large number of households also face an affordability crisis despite the fact the rents have been rising moderately for the past decade. This represents the increasing concentration of low-income households in rental units, due to the selective out-migration to homeownership units of higher-income households.

In sum, we find, in contrast to the Rand study, that a significant number of California households face an affordability problem.

Chapter 3

Supply and Cost of Housing

THE SUPPLY OF HOUSING

In the last fifteen years the California housing market has undergone a substantial set of supply-side changes. New production has been highly cyclical, at times meeting or exceeding demographic demand and at times falling far short of demographic needs because of high interest rates and high unemployment rates that reduce effective household demand. On the average, California has seen the effects of an underproduction of housing relative to household formation in two key ways. First, the relative price of owner-occupied housing has risen dramatically, so that by 1983 it is priced at 70 percent greater than the national average. This relative rise in the price of California housing is in our view due to the impact of local government regulations and controls, local building fees, and to a strong basic demographic demand since the mid-1970s. Very little of the price rise can be attributed to speculation.

The second major effect of the underproduction of housing in California is the extraordinarily low vacancy rate that prevails in coastal metropolitan California. The *for-rent** vacancy rate is about 2 percent, less than one-third of the national average for-rent vacancy rate of 5.8 percent. Both this low vacancy rate number and the rapid rise in relative prices confirm our view that California has an ongoing housing shortage. We now turn to document the problems in the supply of housing in more detail.

NEW CONSTRUCTION

New housing construction can be measured by the number of building permits or housing starts. Both measures show essentially the same picture with only slight differences in timing and the possibility of non-permit usage. Tables 1 and 2 and Figures 1 and 2 show these data since the 1960s for California. Housing starts have varied from over 300,000 units in 1963 to a low of 80,000 units produced in 1982. Average production of new housing units was 196,000 in the 1960s, 210,000 in the 1970s, and 107,000 for the first three years of the 1980s. Since 1975 single family housing has accounted for between 54 and 60 percent of new housing production, multifamily housing for between 25 and 35 percent, and mobile home production for between 8 and 10 percent. In the mid-1960s and early 1970s multi-family production at times represented over one-half of all housing starts. However, the surge towards homeownership, the trend toward rent control, and the curtailment of federal subsidy programs all reduced the building of rental apartments. While new depreciation schedules were put into effect in 1981, rising real rents and low vacancy rates are beginning to encourage more rental apartment building in California. Nonetheless, only a dramatic and comprehensive policy to encourage the building of moderate-income rental housing could change the continual low rental vacancy rate situation in metropolitan California.

In the first four years of the 1980s California new housing

*Unlike the Rand study, we use vacant units for rent rather than all vacant units in our analysis. It is well known that vacant units reported by the Decennial Census (used by Rand) include a substantial overestimate of units available to consumers.

Table 1. California Housing Starts (000)

	All Starts	Single Family	Multifamily	Mobiles
1960	206	120	87	11
1961	212	114	99	9
1962	250	121	130	10
1963	301	132	169	14
1964	256	112	144	15
1965	177	96	81	13
1966	112	72	40	13
1967	111	71	40	10
1968	156	90	66	18
1969	183	84	99	18
1970	172	71	101	17
1971	263	117	145	31
1972	273	129	144	33
1973	214	104	110	25
1974	130	77	54	15
1975	127	87	40	14
1976	204	138	66	18
1977	263	175	87	23
1978	241	145	95	18
1979	211	131	80	15
1980	138	87	51	14
1981	101	60	41	11
1982	80	49	31	7
1983E	160	—	—	—

Note: E = Estimate.
Source: Chase Econometrics/RDA.

production fell over 350,000 units short of basic household formation rates. This shortfall in new production was primarily a result of high mortgage interest rates, which have made it impossible for many households to make their housing demand effective in the market place. This backlog in demand, especially for ownership housing but also for rental housing, is likely to be unleashed when interest rates fall and economic conditions improve. (This is precisely what happened following the recession of 1974 and 1975). The housing recovery of the mid-1980s, is, however, likely to be far more tame than that of the late 1970s—primarily because of the Federal Reserve Board determination to keep real

Table 2. California Housing Permits (000)

	All Permits	Single Family	Multifamily	Mobile Home Shipments
1960	198	125	73	12
1961	214	122	92	9
1962	250	123	127	10
1963	305	129	176	15
1964	258	112	146	16
1965	178	95	83	14
1966	99	65	34	13
1967	110	68	43	11
1968	159	87	72	19
1969	184	80	104	19
1970	195	72	123	18
1971	255	114	141	33
1972	279	126	153	34
1973	216	103	113	27
1974	127	76	51	20
1975	131	90	41	17
1976	220	140	80	21
1977	271	175	96	29
1978	245	144	102	22
1979	211	129	82	18
1980	144	87	58	13
1981	104	60	44	11
1982	85	51	34	8

Source: U.S. Bureau of the Census

interest rates high. In contrast in the late 1970s real interest rates were negative and thus were greatly supportive of the housing market. If we do not have a sharp drop in interest rates, it is likely that the California housing shortfall, despite the recovery in 1983, will continue to accumulate.

NEW AND EXISTING HOME SALES: CHARACTERISTICS OF HOUSES

The new construction market shows a fairly high variance in the size and price of dwellings across metropolitan areas in California. Table 3 shows median and average house prices in

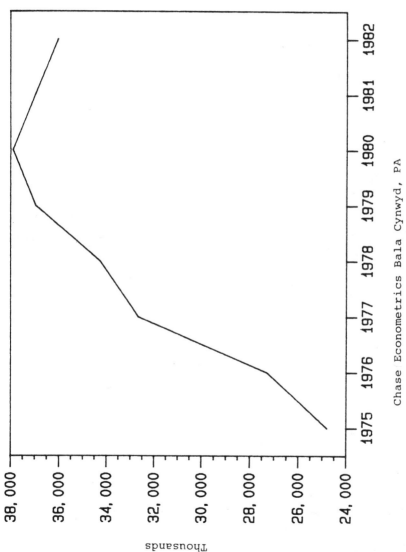

Chase Econometrics Bala Cynwyd, PA

Figure 1. California single-family housing starts, 1966-1982.

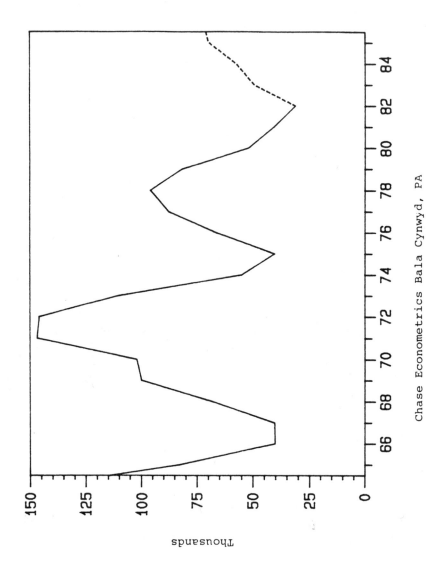

Chase Econometrics Bala Cynwyd, PA

Figure 2. California multifamily housing starts, 1966-1984.

Table 3. Characteristics of New Homes Sold—California and Selected Counties (1982 and Early 1983 Sales)

AREA	Price Median	Price Average	Living Area (Sq. Ft.) Median	Living Area (Sq. Ft.) Average	Price Per Sq. Ft. Median	Price Per Sq. Ft. Average
Selected Counties						
ALAMEDA	$122,000	$132,800	1,507	1,651	$ 80.96	$ 80.44
CONTRA COSTA	147,200	167,200	1,882	1,965	78.21	85.09
FRESNO	70,900	80,800	1,452	1,555	48.83	51.96
KERN	73,500	82,200	1,344	1,465	54.69	56.11
LOS ANGELES	121,700	141,400	1,499	1,660	81.19	85.18
ORANGE	147,500	166,600	1,601	1,744	92.13	95.53
RIVERSIDE	87,100	109,700	1,410	1,487	61.77	73.77
SACRAMENTO	75,000	86,300	1,475	1,546	50.85	55.82
SAN BERNARDINO	70,200	79,600	1,309	1,398	53.63	56.94
SAN DIEGO	111,300	127,100	1,579	1,672	70.49	76.02
SAN FRANCISCO	167,300	180,100	680	826	246.03	218.04
SANTA CLARA	138,200	164,800	1,714	1,849	80.63	89.13
VENTURA	121,200	128,600	1,534	1,659	79.00	77.52
CALIFORNIA	$111,600	$128,500	1,478	1,609	$ 75.51	$ 79.86

Source: Construction Industry Research Board using single-family residential sales data of the California Market Data Cooperative, Inc. A computer analysis of the data was conducted using the Marshall and Swift Market Program computer data base.

living areas for the major housing markets. Prices range from $70,000 in Fresno and San Bernardino to nearly $170,000 in San Francisco. Living areas range in size from 680 square feet in a San Francisco condo to over 1800 square feet in a Contra Costa suburban development. It is clear from these numbers that California has a wide range of housing markets.

Table 4 shows the number and price of resale housing in California since 1970. As Figures 3 and 4 indicate the real price of housing rose dramatically until 1980. Since that time the real price of housing in California has begun to fall slightly. We now turn to an analysis of the cause of the relative rise in housing costs in California.

VACANCY RATES

Table 5 shows estimated multifamily vacancy rates for various metropolitan areas. These vacancy rates are based on a

Table 4. Annual Rate of Resales in California (1970-1982)

Year	Resales	Resale Prices
1970	265,669	24,128
1971	360,730	26,324
1972	425,513	38,479
1973	405,120	31,574
1974	401,342	36,271
1975	454,572	41,100
1976	559,105	52,297
1977	573,244	63,713
1978	604,953	71,281
1979	584,185	82,880
1980	465,186	98,040
1981	332,969	106,040
1982	233,810	110,020
1983E	335,000	113,000

Source: California Association of Realtors and Chase Econometrics/RDA.
Note: E = Estimate.

Table 5. California Vacancy Rates (Multifamily)

County	1979	1980	1981
Alameda	1.5	2.0	1.9
Contra Costa	2.0	3.0	2.3
Fresno	6.1	4.9	5.1
Los Angeles	1.9	2.1	2.4
Marin	2.4	1.7	1.9
Monterey	2.9	2.3	2.1
Orange	2.9	2.7	2.6
Riverside	5.6	7.5	6.2
Sacramento	5.3	4.8	3.8
San Diego	3.7	4.4	3.6
San Francisco	1.2	.8	.7
San Mateo	1.9	2.6	2.1
Santa Clara	1.9	1.5	2.2

Source: Federal Home Loan Bank of San Francisco.

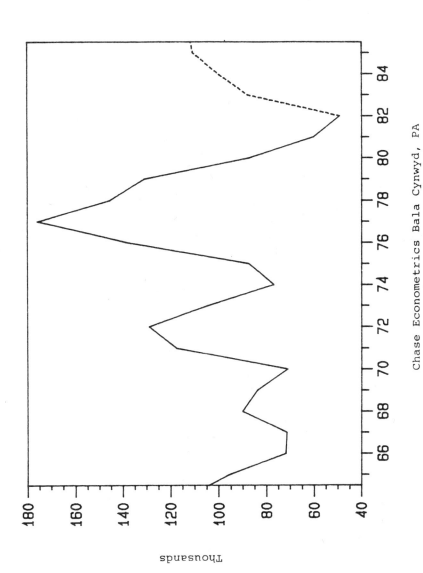

Chase Econometrics Bala Cynwyd, PA

Figure 3. California Association of Realtors real existing median house price in 1967 dollars.

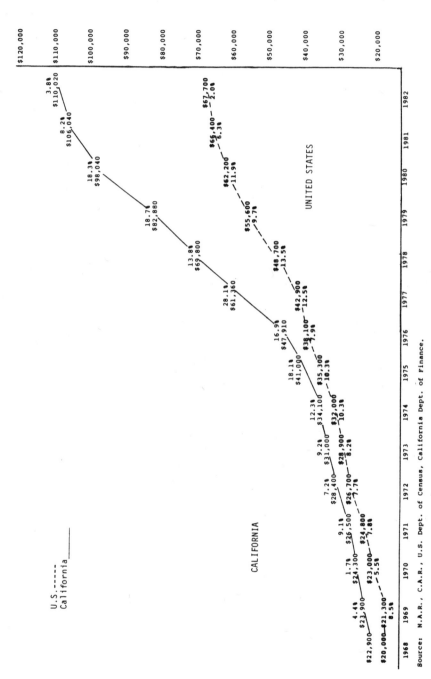

Source: N.A.R., C.A.R., U.S. Dept. of Census, California Dept. of Finance.

Figure 4. Median sales price of existing single-family homes in the United States and California.

postal vacancy survey done by the Federal Home Loan Bank System. They are quite comparable to the "For Rent" vacancy series published quarterly for national and regional data by the Department of Commerce and the Department of Housing. The "For Rent" vacancy series generally is about one-half of the vacancy rate reported in the decennial census. The census numbers are a substantial overestimate of vacancies available for rent. Nearly all analysts thus use the "For Rent" series on a national basis and its postal vacancy proxy on a metropolitan are basis. For most large coastal metropolitan counties vacancy rates were in the 2 to 3 percent range in 1981. San Francisco showed an extremely low vacancy rate of less than 1 percent. Only in three counties did vacancy rates approach 5 percent, a level that would be considered normal for mobility and market efficiency. Thus, these vacancy rate figures indicate that there is a continuing and ongoing shortage of rental housing.

LAND USE CONTROLS AND HOUSING COSTS*

Local policy responses to California housing market problems primarily have been directed at two areas: land-use regulations and rent control. Although these local policies may seem appropriate in the short run, they do not solve the basic problems. Because they tend to inhibit housing production by reducing the ability to meet the demand for housing, in the long run, they are very detrimental.

Local land-use controls take a number of forms—the most common of which are zoning, growth management systems, subdivision regulations, and environmental restrictions. But these regulations, while they seem sound and serve many political purposes, put constraints on the housing market that directly cause housing problems lead to shortages and increased housing prices.

*Portions of the text were taken from Lawrence Katz and Kenneth T. Rosen, "The Effects of Land-Use Controls on Housing Prices" (Berkeley, Calif.: University of California Center for Real Estate and Urban Economics), Working Paper No. 80-13.

It is a fairly well-known fact that California in general and the San Francisco and Los Angeles areas in particular have house prices that are the highest in the country, exceeding the national median by over 70 percent. What is not well-known, however, is that less than ten years ago California house prices were at the national median. This dramatic surge has coincided with three other phenomenon: a large increase in net migration to California from the rest of the country, a surge in household formations reflecting the maturation of the post World War II baby boom, and a massive increase in the use of land-use and growth-management techniques to slow and stop new housing production. While we contend that there is a direct causal relationship between all these factors and the sharp relative acceleration in California house prices, the most important element by far in the house price rise is the stringent land-use regulations that have been imposed in the mid- and late-1970s.

Table 6 shows the large difference in land costs between California and other parts of the country. Land costs per square foot are nearly twice as high in California as anywhere else in the country and are triple that of states with average land costs, such as Texas. An average tiny California lot costs nearly $36,000 dollars, or nearly $190,000 per acre! This compares with a lot of $14,000 to $18,000 ($55,000 per acre) elsewhere in the country. A response to this high cost of land is that California lots are typically less than one-fifth of an acre, about one-third less than the U.S. average. Even with this smaller lot size, land costs comprise 37 percent of the value of new homes in California, versus 22 percent nationally. As Table 6 also reveals, this high cost of developed lots is not caused by the high price of rural farm land. California farm land values are above average but are still below values in places such as Illinois and New Jersey. It is also not caused by such factors as population density, higher income, or more compact urban areas, as many eastern states surpass California in these statistics. In our view, the main explanation for these higher-developed lot costs is local land-use regulations.

A further confirmation of this view is illustrated in Table 7. This table shows land and housing prices in 1976 and 1981 and the

Table 6. Land Costs (1981)

	Average Cost of Lot	Average Cost of Lot Per Square Foot (Dollars)	Average Cost of Lot Per Acre (Dollars)	Average Size of Lot (Acres)	Average Value of Farm Land Per Acre (Dollars)	Average Sales Price of House (Dollars)
California	35,500	4.39	190,860	.186	1,546	96,151
Colorado	17,366	2.31	100,381	.173	365	76,230
Florida	15,769	1.58	68,860	.229	1,368	65,726
Georgia	11,405	.65	28,160	.405	769	62,893
Illinois	16,888	1.28	55,552	.304	1,960	79,209
Michigan	14,077	.85	37,142	.379	956	66,604
Missouri	14,765	1.32	57,228	.258	803	75,581
New Jersey	19,054	1.34	58,269	.327	2,306	76,684
Texas	17,972	2.02	88,098	.204	448	67,693
Virginia	18,076	1.74	75,631	.239	846	75,825

Source: Derived from Proprietary Builder Survey and Department of Agriculture.

Table 7. Land Costs and Housing Costs (1976 and 1981)

	Average Cost of Lot-Dollars Per Square Foot			Average Cost of House-Dollars Per Square Foot		
	1976	1981	% Change	1976	1981	% Change
California	1.57	4.39	179.6	36.01	52.74	46.5
Colorado	.95	2.31	143.1	27.43	48.15	75.5
Florida	.95	1.58	66.3	28.85	40.69	41.0
Georgia	.45	.65	44.4	31.99	36.63	14.5
Illinois	1.09	1.28	17.4	34.04	49.60	45.7
Michigan	.72	.85	18.1	30.93	43.19	39.6
Missouri	.79	1.32	67.1	29.01	42.05	44.9
New Jersey	.79	1.34	69.6	31.27	40.81	30.5
Texas	.69	2.02	192.7	24.34	38.83	59.5
Virginia	.87	1.74	100.0	31.95	44.11	38.1

Source: Derived from Proprietary Builder Survey.

percentage change over this period. It shows a level and percentage increase in land costs in California that is nearly double those in most other parts of the country. It was precisely during this period that land-use controls were becoming increasingly prevalent in California. A more rigorous econometric analysis of the cost of land-use controls in the San Francisco Bay Area in 1979 indicates that growth moratoria and growth control plans have raised prices between 18 and 28 percent in those areas where they are present. (See Katz and Rosen, "The Effects of Land-Use Controls on Housing Prices.")

PROPOSITION 13 AND THE SHIFT OF DEVELOPMENT FEES TO THE NEW HOME BUYER

While stringent land-use controls are a major cause of high house prices in California, other factors have also played a role. The passage of Proposition 13 has led a number of communities to attempt to shift the public costs normally associated with new housing development to the new homebuyer. There are fifteen cities in the San Francisco Bay Area that have development fees exceeding $5,000 per unit. This of course raises the price of new housing by 5 to 10 percent before a shovel of dirt is turned. As Table 8 illustrates, the fees range from $1,321 in San Mateo to over $8,143 in Livermore.

If we combine higher land costs with these development fees it is quite clear that $25,000 of the price differential of $40,000 between California and the rest of the nation can be explained by these two factors. Thus, we would strongly disagree with the Rand conclusion that "speculation" alone has caused high California house prices. Rather, it is land-use controls and local government regulations and fees that explain much of the differential. Higher California incomes and strong demographic demand probably account for the remainder of the differential with "speculation" playing only a minor role.

**Table 8. Per Unit Development Fees in Bay Area
           Communities (1981)**

Livermore	$8,143
Tiburon	8,568
Fairfield	8,269
Suisun City	6,631
Vacaville	6,190
Vallejo	6,451
Morgan Hill	6,031
Pleasanton	5,999
Antioch	5,536
Union City	5,575
Pacifica	5,672
Los Gatos	5,775
San Jose	6,401
Dixon	5,041
San Mateo	1,321

Source: Association of Bay Area Governments.

RENTAL HOUSING SUPPLY
PROBLEM*

Rent control became a popular form of local regulation as a result of housing shortages in many urban metropolitan areas, generally low vacancy rates, and a perception, on the part of consumers and politicians, that rents were rising very rapidly. In fact rents in the 1970s failed (by a wide margin) to keep pace with general price rises.

The rental housing problem centers on the problem of inadequate returns, which have not risen enough to cover increased construction and operating costs while still providing a return to investors in rental housing comparable to that available elsewhere in the economy. However, since rental costs comprise a high and growing percentage of low- and lower-middle-income household budgets, even modest rent increases appear very large relative to their increase in income. Unable to "vote with their feet" because of

*Portions of the text taken from Kenneth R. Rosen, *Housing and Mortgage Policies in the 1980s* (New York: 20th Century Fund, 1984), forthcoming.

low vacancy rates, renters have increasingly turned to the political system for rent control regulations.

The increased interest in rent control has been spurred by recent trends in the rental housing market. Between 1965 and 1974 rental vacancy rates experienced a drastic decline. Not even the construction boom of the early 1970s could greatly alter this trend. Since 1974 vacancy rates have continued to decline in many areas, especially those with operational or contemplated rent control programs. In such metropolitan areas as Los Angeles, San Francisco, and San Diego, the rental vacancy rate has fallen well below the 5 percent rate typically considered the minimum necessary in a normally functioning housing market.

Despite tight markets, private supply response has been slow. This has been attributed to divergent trends in income, prices, and costs in rental markets since the mid-1960s. These trends have created a situation in which rental housing is simultaneously less profitable to investors and less affordable to some classes of renters.

On the cost side, the median gross rent rose 7 percent per year in the 1970s and early 1980s. This compares with a rise in renter median income of 8 percent over the same period. At the same time, the overall inflation rate in the economy rose 8 percent and construction costs rose over 8.7 percent. These data indicate the divergent trends in costs, prices, and income in the past decade. This has created a rental price-income squeeze for some tenants (though most tenants are better off) and a construction cost-rental price squeeze for builders. In order to increase new production, the rental price would have to rise faster than the income of tenants. These divergent trends have created a major dilemma for policymakers. They also explain such phenomena as the spread of rent control in the face of relatively slowly rising rents. While a good explanation has never been offered for these divergent trends, it is apparent that the income of tenants, because of an increasing concentration of low-income households in rental units, would not support the rent increases necessary to meet new construction costs. Thus, the extremely tight rental supply in many areas of the state due to the lack of new construction is not likely to be resolved without a dramatic increase in tenant income. Low-income tenants on relatively fixed incomes are seeing their rent/income ratios rise and are also experiencing the decreased purchasing power of the remainder of their income.

This trend is partially due to the self-selection process. Former tenants who increasingly have opted to purchase their own homes have been at the higher end of the renter-income distribution. Therefore, the remaining occupants of rental units exhibit a higher proportion of low-income households: the percentage of households paying over 35 percent of their income for rent was over 32 percent in 1980. These facts substantiate the possibility of a growing housing affordability problem for renters, even though rents are not rising as fast as the prices of other goods.

Landlords and developers see this situation in quite a different light, whereby the cost of constructing and operating a unit has risen relative to rental income, making it unprofitable to build nonsubsidized rental housing units. This trend has created a cost-price gap of over 30 percent in many parts of the state. Cash flow is frequently negative, and even with appreciation in property values, rental housing is a difficult investment to justify in comparison to alternatives. Rents would have to rise from 25 to 40 percent in most parts of the state to make a rental housing project economically acceptable.

Another aspect of the rental supply problem is the trend toward converting rental units into owner-occupied condominium or co-operative units. Landlords facing a rental rate of return far below market levels find that they can achieve a higher return by liquidating rental real estate investments. The high demand for these homeowner units is a very clear incentive for landlords. Although this depletes the rental housing stock, it also has the benefit of adding to the lower-cost, owner-occupied housing stock, thereby allowing more young and lower-income households to become first-time homebuyers. However, the rental housing shortage is approaching critical dimensions in many parts of the state. The vacancy rate is near its lowest point in twenty years. This renders mobility far more difficult. Renters tend to remain stationary, while those who are forced to move are likely to encounter fairly substantial rent increases and a tightening housing market.

Under these circumstances rent control seems attractive to renters and politicians, but it does not attack the real problem— a shortage of affordable housing. Ultimately, this housing shortage and affordability crisis can only be resolved by the construction of an adequate number of affordable housing units. Not only does rent control fail to provide new construction incentives, it almost certainly discourages new construction and other forms of supply expansion.

THE RENT CONTROL DEBATE

The volume of arguments against rent control make its seeming popularity inexplicable. Rent control reduces the supply of new rental housing by reducing net yields relative to other investments, and it encourages the conversion of existing rental units into cooperatives and condominiums.

Rents below market level create excess demand for rental housing. Faced with an excess demand for their units and unable to raise rents, landlords often reduce maintenance and defer repairs to preserve profit margins without fear of losing tenants. When costs rise, inability to raise rents or reduce fixed capital expenditures induce landlords to curtail maintenance and repair expenditures, which reduces the quality of rental housing units and leads to a faster depreciation of the housing stock. In the long run, this leads to increased abandonments and neighborhood blight.

Rent control leads to an erosion of the local tax base by decreasing the value of rental housing properties. By reducing the income-producing ability of rental properties, rent control necessarily reduces the value of these properties. Value is also reduced because of reduced maintenance and repairs and neighborhood effects, which cause a decrease in the value of surrounding properties. The erosion of the urban tax base can lead to a reduction in municipal expenditures, which usually reduces the benefit to the urban poor the most. A shift in property tax away from rental housing owners and onto homeowners and businesses is another result.

Rent control creates severe inequities among tenants. Many well-to-do tenants who have little or no need for regulatory protection are beneficiaries of these programs. Tenants in rent-controlled units are able to reap the benefits of lower rents simply by virtue of already residing in the units. Others must either compete for the few, if any, controlled units that become available or pay the higher, uncontrolled market rents.

Policymakers describe programs that indiscriminantly distribute benefits as lacking in "target efficiency;" they are poorly aimed or directed. Most California rent control systems fail to benefit those who most need help, since they are designed to favor long-term tenants and tend to exclude the poor who tend to be more highly mobile. This aspect of rent control also reduces the mobility of the labor force, since moving in order to get a better-paying job may not be profitable if the tradeoff is a higher rent.

Other economic inefficiencies that may result are the misallocation of housing space and the reduction in new construction. When newly constructed dwellings are exempted, many tenants, particularly older ones, may find it cheaper to remain in large, older, controlled units rather than to move into smaller units adequate for their needs. Since institutional lenders avoid units under rent control, the availability of mortgage credit for multi-family rental projects is limited in areas subject to this regulation.

Aside from its direct effects on the housing market, rent control has many shortfalls from an administrative standpoint. These programs are expensive to administer since they deal with numerous, relatively small business entities whose financial circumstances vary and whose ability to pay for or use technical assistance is often severely limited. Finally, even when temporary controls may be justified in a serious emergency, rent control is often extremely difficult to eliminate once introduced.

THE EFFECTS OF RENT CONTROL OF NEW CONSTRUCTION AND THE EXISTING HOUSING STOCK

Since rent control is often imposed to counter price effects of a housing shortage, its effect on the construction of new rental housing units is a matter of considerable interest. Rather than helping to alleviate housing shortages, rent controls, by discouraging investment in new rental housing and encouraging the conversion of rental housing into other forms of occupancy, tend to create shortages where they did not previously exist and to make existing shortages even more severe.

A fairly large body of literature indicates that restrictive rent controls have discouraged new construction by the private sector.* While there is almost universal agreement that long-term restrictive rent control leads to serious declines in new construction, the proponents of rent control argue that moderate rent controls do not have a negative impact on investments in rental housing since new construction is often excluded from regulation and since landlords are allowed what proponents describe as a "fair return." It can be shown, however, that even moderate rent control leads to a substantial decline in new construction.

Expected profit from rental investment is a function of six key variables: expected occupancy rates, rental prices, construction costs, operating costs, revenues from reduction of tax liabilities of the investor (depreciation), and capital gains from holding the property. By reducing rents below what they otherwise would have been, rent control reduces the expected revenue of rental housing projects and the expected profitability of such ventures. Likewise, expected capital gains are reduced with rent control because of the lower values of future revenues and the more rapid deterioration of the physical structure. Lower operating (maintenance and repair) costs and higher occupancy rates produced by rent control, both of which add to expected profits, work in the opposite direction.

The possibility that rent control will be made more restrictive or be extended to other areas in the future serves to increase the riskiness of rental housing investments. This increased risk reduces expected profit by decreasing the expected rental revenue flow and in turn translates directly into the reduced supply of

---

*W. Block and E. Olsen, *Rent Control: Myths and Realities* (Vancouver: The Fraser Institute, 1981).

new construction, as new rental housing construction depends heavily on the profitability of such investments.

Econometric studies indicated that new rental construction is highly responsive to rate of return. These studies generally show that rental housing starts rise when rents increase (leading to higher return on investment) and fall when an increase in construction costs and operating costs cause a decline in expected returns. They show a highly sensitive housing supply system (the price elasticity of new starts with respect to real rents varies from 5 to 14 between regions).

One additional variable can significantly influence the speed of adjustment and hence the supply of new construction—the availability of mortgage and construction financing, a necessary input into most new projects. These results imply that, even if developers are willing to build in rent-controlled communities, rent control can still have a negative influence on new construction if its uncertainty-generating effects cause lenders to reduce the availability of mortgage funds for new rental housing.

There are special situations in which rent control may not depress new construction. During a recession, rent restrictions may become nonbinding so that they have no direct effect on supply. When growth controls or zoning are so rigid or stringent as to prevent a supply response even in the absence of rent control, rent control itself will not affect new construction.

The effects of rent control on the existing housing stock are analogous to those on new construction. As rent control depresses the rate of return on the existing stock of houses, it encourages landlords to make calculations similar to those of investors. They can be expected to take short-term actions to restore pre-control profits and/or disinvest at an early opportunity. The rental housing stock will eventually deteriorate both qualitatively and quantitatively, as it has in a number of European countries that have had rent control in effect for an extended period of time.

The best way to encourage new construction and an adequate supply and maintenance of existing stock is to raise the rate of return to a point where it is more in line with the overall market rate of return. A profit shortfall is the problem the market has been facing for the past five years. Rent control has not solved this problem but has only served to worsen the situation.

Chapter 4

Restructuring of the California Housing Finance System*

The late 1970s and early 1980s saw major restructuring of the traditional housing finance system. Regulation of deposit interest rates at financial institutions has been virtually eliminated. New types of deposit accounts calculated to restore savings flows to thrifts have become common. Secondary market transactions and pass-through certificates, whereby mortgage originators sell their loans to nontraditional mortgage lenders, are increasingly used as tools to generate cash, which, in turn, can be used to originate additional mortgages. An array of new mortgage instruments, such as adjustable rate, graduated payment, and growing equity loans that take into account variations in household life cycle and income circumstances, are now an important supplement to the traditional fixed-rate,fixed-payment mortgage.

These innovations have arisen in an environment characterized by periodic bouts of disintermediation, the mortgage credit gap,

---

*Portions of the text were taken from Kenneth R. Rosen, *Housing and Mortgage Policies in the 1980s* (New York: 20th Century Fund, 1984), forthcoming.

the affordability crisis for first-time buyers, the profitability crisis for lenders, and volatile interest rates. They represent a large change in institutional priorities and policies.

DEREGULATIONS OF THE DEPOSIT MARKET

The major characteristic of the consumer deposit market from 1965 to 1978 was the fairly rigid interest rate ceilings placed on deposit accounts. Under Regulation Q and related provisions, the maximum interest rate that thrift institutions and commercial banks could pay on passbook and term deposits was set by the agency responsible for regulating them. In the late 1970s, however, this highly regulated financial structure began to look increasingly vulnerable. High and volatile interest and inflation rates, combined with rigid deposit interest rate ceilings, made deposits at regulated financial institutions unattractive. The sophistication of depositors seemed to grow with each increase in market interest rates. Investments in Treasury bills and money market mutual funds became increasingly common. The major negative consequences of the ceilings fell increasingly on unsophisticated, often elderly, savers. As disintermediation proceeded, the inequity of this Regulation Q tax became more and more apparent to both the public and politicians.

The initial response of regulators to the eroding effectiveness of Regulation Q ceilings was piecemeal deregulation. In a classic case of price discrimination, ceilings on short-term, larger-deposit accounts were relaxed. In June 1978 regulated financial institutions were first authorized to offer money market certificates (MMCs) with interest rates tied to the rate determined at the most recent six-month Treasury bill auction. Until March 1979 thrift institutions continued to pay 0.25 percent more than commercial banks; since then, the differential has been eliminated when the Treasury bill rate is above 9 percent.

In January 1980, financial institutions were also authorized to offer variable-ceiling deposits with maturities of two and one half years or more ("small savers certificates," or SSCs). In March

1980 a temporary ceiling interest rate of 12 percent was placed on these accounts—effectively making them a below-market account. In August 1981 they were fully deregulated.

Finally, with the introduction of the money market deposit account in December 1982, regulated financial institution were allowed to offer market rates on virtually all short-term deposits. The MMDA accounts had no interest rate ceiling and allowed depositors to write a maximum of three checks per month—making them quite similar to money market mutual funds.

Judged by consumer acceptance, the MMC, SSC, MMDA, and NOW accounts have been major successes. By March 1983 nearly 75 percent of all thrift deposits were in these accounts. Table 1 shows the distribution of thrift deposits by account type in 1978 and 1983.

CHANGING SOURCES OF MORTGAGE CREDIT

Deregulation of the deposit market has had a large effect on the role of traditional lenders in the mortgage market. There has been a dramatic shift within the institutional lending community in terms of *net* mortgage extension (change in net holdings of mortgages). Table 2 shows the drop in the savings and loan mortgage market share, the sharp rise in the role of the secondary market transactions (represented by FNMA and FHLMC), and the role of commercial banks. This table also shows the small but increasing role in the mortgage market plays in state and local government agencies through CHFA and Cal-Vet loans. The reduction in the savings and loan market share of all mortgage lending results from a declining share of consumer deposits and from recent Federal Home Loan Bank actions easing restrictions on the savings and loan asset portfolio. These short-term phenomena are highlighted further by Table 3, which shows mortgage closings by lender. Here both the substantial rise in the role of mortgage bankers in California and the decline in the role of savings and loans are demonstrated.

The mortgage market will adjust to the diminishing role of sav-

Table 1. Distribution of Savings Deposits by Type— Eleventh Federal Home Loan Bank District[a] (Billions of $)

	March 31, 1983	March 31, 1978
Short-Term Deposits		
Money Market Deposit	31.536	—
Passbook Accounts	11.757	24.661
NOW	2.056	—
Super NOW	2.016	—
Six-Month Money Market	19.291	—
Jumbo CDs	24.272	4.016
Long-Term Deposits		
Small Savers Certificate	18.196	—
3½ year	2.985	—
No ceiling fixed	1.861	—
All-savers	.707	—
Other fixed	5.093	40.479
Total all deposits	121.780	69.157

Source: Federal Home Loan Bank of San Francisco: Semi-Annual Reports.
[a]Over 90 percent of deposit liabilities in this district are in California.

Table 2. Stock of Mortgage Loans Held[a] (Millions of Dollars)

	Savings and Loan	Commercial Banks	Federal National Mortgage Association	Federal Home Loan Mortgage Corporation	California Housing Finance Agency	Cal-Vet
1970	28,250	7,076	2,456	—	—	1,241
1971	31,906	8,221	2,773	—	—	1,194
1972	37,199	9,678	3,024	—	—	1,147
1973	41,116	11,843	3,848	—	—	1,237
1974	43,801	12,734	5,046	—	—	1,330
1975	49,099	11,681	5,782	—	—	1,369
1976	58,517	12,144	5,757	—	100	1,391
1977	70,736	15,268	6,477	2,026	100	1,461
1978	80,767	19,096	9,332	5,090	275	1,583
1979	92,516	23,986	11,695	8,260	615	1,953
1980	98,192	27,734	13,783	10,413	645	2,316
1981	103,236	29,796	15,050	11,910	915	2,571
1982	104,160	30,650	16,771	16,558	1,335	2,738

Source: Federal Home Loan Bank San Francisco, CHFA, Chase Econometrics/RDA, California Department of Veterans Affairs.
[a]No regional breakdown of GNMA loans were available, our best estimate in that GNMA passthroughs account for 30 billion in mortgages held in 1982.

Table 3. California Mortgage Loans Closed (Millions of Dollars)

	All Institutional Lenders	Savings and Loans	Mortgage Bankers	Commercial Banks[a]
1970	3,768	1,654	—	—
1971	6,659	3,059	—	1,845
1972	9,075	4,654	2,142	2,279
1973	11,063	4,540	3,391	3,132
1974	9,312	3,900	3,337	2,075
1975	9,852	5,821	3,811	220
1976	16,054	9,907	4,516	1,631
1977	23,999	13,534	6,126	4,339
1978	26,896	13,513	8,029	5,354
1979	29,766	15,277	7,689	6,800
1980	21,281	9,170	5,964	6,147
1981	14,011	4,513	4,663	4,835
1982	13,385	3,740	5,812	3,833

[a]Estimated by taking first difference of mortgage stock and assuming a 10 percent repayment rate.

ings and loans in mortgage originations in a number of ways. Mortgage rates will be driven up because of the excess demand conditions. As a result, the credit gap is likely to produce higher relative mortgage interest rates and lower loan-to-value ratios (higher downpayment requirements). More attractive mortgage terms should induce nonthrift institutions to make more mortgage loans. Thus, pension funds and life insurance companies will increasingly purchase the attractively priced new mortgages as they become available. Thrift institutions themselves will alter their behavior if normal sources of cash flow are insufficient to meet mortgage demand. In particular, thrifts will increase borrowing from the Federal Home Loan Banks System and other sources, including mortgage-backed bonds. A strong continued movement toward secondary market sales is likely, both in a direct form and through "mortgage pool" or pass-through securities. This trend, in which the ultimate holders of mortgages are different from the originators, is likely to accelerate in the 1980s. It will be accommodated in part by the role of the quasi-federal agencies as guarantors of these mortgage pools.

CREATIVE FINANCING*

In addition to these institutional adjustments, there have also been major adjustments by homebuyers, sellers, and builders to the new mortgage realities of the 1980s. There has been a phenomenal growth of "creative financing" arrangements in California. While the term "creative financing" can be applied to a number of alternative financing techniques, we confine ourselves to three major mechanisms used in the early 1980s and still used to some extent today. The first is the "buydown" of mortgage interest rates for a two- to five-year period by a new homebuilder. Thus, the builder can reduce his buyer's cost for a period of time by paying the interest for the buyer to the financial institution. Presumably, after this period of time the borrower's income will rise (because of inflation) so that he or she could afford market rate financing.

The second major mechanism concerns the financing of existing houses through the assumption (transfer) of an existing low-rate mortgage loan by the buyer from the seller. The third mechanism involves the provision by the seller of a first, second, and/or third mortgage loan, often at below-market rates. The extent of these techniques for financing existing home sales has been estimated to be as high as 75 percent of all 1981 transactions in California. By 1983, however, the share of creative financing had fallen to less than 40 percent.

The Extent of Creative Financing

Measuring the extent of the use of creative financing in California housing markets is not a straightforward task. Several different techniques, have been used. The first is the survey technique in which a sample of home transactions is constructed. The California

---

*Portions of the text were taken from Kenneth T. Rosen "Creative Financing and Housing Prices: A Study of Capitalization Effects" (Berkeley, Calif.: University of California Center for Real Estate and Urban Economics), Working Paper No. 82-52.

Association of Realtors, the National Association of Realtors, and the Rand corporation all conducted such surveys. These surveys yielded valuable information on the type and characteristics of creative financing transactions at the time of the survey. However, because of the difficulty in expanding small samples to the universe of all transactions, none of these surveys can be used to determine the aggregate amount of creative financing.

Therefore, we have used an alternative methodology to compute the amount of creative financing. Our technique first calculates the total dollar value of housing transactions. This is done by taking total home sales and multiplying average house prices times average loan-to-value ratio. This is done only for the resale housing market. It provides an estimate of the total demand for financing in the state. We then subtract from these numbers the dollar amount of institutional mortgage originations (from savings and loans, commercial banks, and mortgage bankers) to determine the amount of mortgage assumptions and seller financing that has occurred. The percentage and dollar amounts are normalized by the average percentage of noninstitutional financing for the 1970 through 1978 period. While this is a somewhat complicated methodology, the results give a fairly accurate measure of the amount of nontraditional financing. Table 4 presents our dollar estimates of creative financing by type for California. It also presents a comparison of our estimates with those implicit in the California Association of Realtors (C.A.R.) and Rand studies. We estimate that $16 billion of creative financing occurred in the last five years.

It is quite clear from this chart that the use of creative financing skyrocketed in the early 1980s. Over 60 percent of the value of home sales were being financed creatively in California. This compares with a normal value of 20 percent. These estimates are quite consistent with the C.A.R. survey which shows a 70 percent incidence of creative financing and the Nation Association of Realtors (N.A.R.) survey, which shows a 60 percent incidence of creative financing in terms of the number of transactions.

Our results, however, show a much smaller dollar amount of aggregate creative financing than the Rand study. The Rand study makes a major error in its assumption that the percentage of cre-

Table 4. Creative Financing in California for Existing Homes, 1978-1982 (Billions of Dollars)

	Institutional Mortgage Originations	Adjusted[a] Market Value of Home Sales	Amount Creatively Financed	C.A.R. Estimate Creative Financing	Rand Estimate Creative Financing
1978	18.690	19.016	0.326	—	—
1979	20.126	21.177	1.051	—	—
1980	13.944	20.254	6.310	8.685	—
1981	9.314	15.583	6.269	10.188	26.0
1982	8.897	11.009	2.112	7.000	—
Total	—	—	16.068	25.873	

Source: Derived from C.A.R. and Rand data.
[a]Adjusted by the average of institutional and creative financing for the 1970 through 1978 period.

ative financing was constant at the 1981 peak level throughout the 1978 to 1982 period. As Table 4 shows, this assumption is completely unjustified.

Creative Financing and House Prices

The widespread presence of creative financing in the early 1980s has had a substantial impact on house prices. It is our view that a household purchasing a home with favorable creative financing is purchasing not only the house with all its physical and locational characteristics but is also purchasing a package of financing from the seller. Since the buyer is receiving an assumable first mortgage and/or a seller second mortgage below current market rates, the buyer should be willing to pay, and the seller should demand a price premium for a sale that includes favorable financing. The amount of the premium will vary depending on the present value of the savings over current market financing that the favorable financing package provides. In general, the lower the interest rate and the longer the term of the financing package, the more valuable the package will be. Adding to these favorable terms is the fact that, in most cases, the buyer of a

house with creative financing avoids stringent institutional qualifying criteria. Thus, buyers who might otherwise be considered
"marginal" from the financial institutions' viewpoint can obtain
financing in this fashion.

Offsetting these positive effects on price are several other factors. A creatively financed home purchase might involve a larger
downpayment from the buyer, as a significant portion of the old
low-rate loan might have already been paid off. Everything else
equal, this would tend to lower the creative finance price premium.
Second, a creative financing package with a balloon second due in
one to three years might be considered risky by the buyer and so,
despite a concessionary interest rate, might command a smaller
price premium. Finally, since mortgage interest payments are tax-
deductible, taxpayers in high marginal tax brackets will not value
savings from a creative financing package as highly as if these
were no interest tax deduction.

Given the array of factors that may influence the "creative
finance price premium," it would be a mistake to *assume* that a
direct adjustment (based on the present discounted value of the
cash savings from the financing package—known as the cash equiv-
alence method in the appraisal literature) to the sales price would
be appropriate. In fact, our own statistical analysis, based on
actual market transactions, implies that the cash-equivalent method
is a good first approximation of the appraisal adjustment required
for creative financing. It thus appears that the market, at least
in our data sample, values creative financing at its present discounted cash value, with the buyer paying a full creative financing
premium for this financing package.

Thus, based on statistical work, if creative financing were not
available, the selling price of the average house that was creatively financed in 1980, 1981, and 1982 in California would be
reduced by 9.8 percent.* This aggregate adjustment must be contrasted with the disaggregate adjustment that would result from
the individual terms of each transaction.

---

*Using an econometric analysis, Rosen (op.cit.) separated the price effects of creative
financing from the other elements of the package of goods and services that typically
comprise a house sales.

Using the data in our earlier chart, we can then apply this discount to the proportion of the value of transactions using creative financing. We also assume that prior to 1979 creative financing did not involve substantial savings to the borrower, and thus no price correction is necessary. Table 5 shows the actual and corrected price series in 1980, 1981, and 1982. The creative finance premium in the aggregate California house price series is thus estimated to be 3.9 percent in 1980, 3.7 percent in 1981, and 3.2 percent in 1982. Since over 80 percent of the premium is due to the assumption of a first mortgage, the recent decision confirming the enforcement of the due on sale clause, if applied fully to California data, would reduce *reported* sales prices by approximately 3.2 percent relative to an assumable mortgage environment. This small price adjustment is far from the massive "watering of prices" that the Rand study claims has occurred. Their claim that one-fourth of all houses in California have a debt to equity ratio over 1 is just not supported by the empirical evidence.

Is There a Creative Financing Problem?

Rand estimates that $36 billion of seller financing in California is outstanding, with $24 billion of balloon loans coming due in the next four years. On the other hand, C.A.R. estimates that only $17 billion of seller loans were written during the entire period.

Reviewing our empirical work and considering the fact that mortgage money is plentiful and available at a rate between 10.5 percent (on adjustable loans) and 13.5 percent (fixed rate loans), it is our view that there is no creative financing crisis.

NEW MORTGAGE INSTRUMENTS: A SOLUTION TO THE BUYERS' AND LENDERS' PROBLEMS*

In the spring of 1981 major changes in the type of mortgage instruments allowed by federal-chartered financial institu-

---

*Portions of this section were taken from Kenneth R. Rosen "New Mortgage Instruments: A Solution to the Buyers' and Lenders' Problems", Berkeley, Calif.: University of California Center for Real Estate and Urban Economics), Working Paper No. 81-34.

Table 5. California House Price Appreciation (Adjusted for Creative Financing)

Year	Rate of Appreciation Existing Homes	Creative Finance Adjustment to Base Prices	Creative Finance Adjustments to Appreciation Rate	"True" Price Appreciation
1975	20.2	—	—	20.2
1976	11.6	—	—	11.6
1977	27.9	—	—	27.9
1978	13.7	—	—	13.7
1979	18.6	—	—	18.6
1980	18.4	—3.9	—3.9	14.5
1981	8.1	—3.7	+0.2	8.3
1982	3.7	—3.2	+0.7	4.4

Source: Raw data for prices from California Association of Realtors. (Corrections calculated by author).

tions were authorized by federal regulatory action. In March of 1981 the comptroller of the currency allowed national banks to make an adjustable rate mortgage (ARM) loan in which interest rates could be raised or lowered, according to a change in a specified index, by 1 percent every six months (2 percent per year). There was no limit on the cumulative change in interest rates over the life of the loan. In April 1981 Richard Pratt, the newly appointed chairman of the Federal Home Loan Bank Board and a strong advocate of free market principals, far exceeded the comptroller's efforts of a month before and completely deregulated the mortgage instrument. He authorized the adjustable loan (AML), in which no limits are placed on payments or interest rate adjustments on an annual or cumulative basis. Any index readily verifiable by consumers and outside of the control of the lender could be used for interest rate or payment adjustments. In July 1981 the FHLBB also authorized a combined graduated payment and adjustable mortgage loan with no limit on negative amortization. In March 1983 the comptroller of the currency issued new regulations for national banks allowing them to use any interest rate index upon which to base their adjustable rate mortgage indexes. These new ARM regulations also removed all limits on periodic or aggregate changes to interest or monthly payment amounts.

The revolution that these three changes in federal regulations are bringing forth in the housing finance system cannot be underestimated. Prior to this time, only limited experimentation with alternative mortgages was allowed. Only the graduated payment mortgage and several highly constrained versions in the variable rate mortgage were in use. The new mortgage instruments are bringing about a resurrection of the housing finance system.

We now proceed to briefly examine the rationale for new mortgage instruments and each major new instrument type in detail.

RATIONALE FOR NEW MORTGAGE LOAN INSTRUMENTS

The fixed payment-fixed interest rate mortgage which has been the mainstay of the housing finance system for nearly thirty years, has, in the present environment of volatile and high interest rates and inflation created a serious "profitability crisis" for lenders and an "affordability crisis" for homebuyers. In this type of economic environment, the fixed payment-fixed interest rate mortgage serves neither the borrower nor the lender well.

On the lender's side, the main impetus for change has come from changes in federal regulations of deposit interest rates. These changes assure that the 1980s will be a decade in which the depository institutions will be forced to compete for liabilities in a deregulated environment. The introduction of new deposit accounts means that the financial institutions have to pay market rates for nearly all liabilities.

While deposit rate flexibility on all maturity classes has created a competitive deposit market, a key issue concerns the ability of financial institutions to pay market returns on assets without causing massive failures of institutions. The only way financial institutions can afford to pay market rates on liabilities is if they are also allowed to receive market rates on all their assets. As a result, the movement toward market rates on liabilities has required regulators to introduce fully variable rate mortgage instruments. Thus, from the lender's perspective, a fully variable rate mortgage is essential to lenders with a fully variable rate liability structure.

From the borrower's perspective, high inflation rates have also made the fixed payment-fixed interest mortgage outdated. The interest rate on the mortgage loan is crucially affected by the rate of inflation. The mortgage interest rate is a function of both the expected inflation rate and the real interest component. The high inflation rates of the early 1980s have raised the contract interest rate and have thus raised the monthly carrying costs of a conventional mortgage by over 100 percent. Compared with a 1 to 2 percent inflation world, the present monthly carrying costs of a conventional mortgage are over *five times* higher than would be expected in a low-inflation economy. This rise in mortgage payments, and the corresponding rise in the initial yearly payments/income, led to the development of alternative instruments that could alleviate many problems for most lenders and borrowers.

DESCRIPTION OF NEW MORTGAGE LOAN INSTRUMENTS

There are essentially two major classes of new mortgage loans (other than the fixed rate-fixed payment loan) that will be used by the mortgage market in the 1980s. The first type is the variable rate mortgage, which includes the adjustable mortgage loan, the adjustable rate mortgage, the rollover mortgage, and the renegotiable rate mortgage. In all these instruments the interest rate can be adjusted based on the movement of a market interest rate index. The second type of new mortgage is the graduated payment mortgage (actually authorized in 1977), in which payments in the early years of a loan are substantially lower than those necessary to amortize the loan and in which payments rise gradually at a preset rate for a number of years.

Variable Rate Mortgages (VRM)

Federal regulations had in essence created two types of variable rate mortgages from the period from 1981 to 1983. The comptroller's regulations, which apply to national banks, had created an adjustable-rate mortgage loan known as an ARM. The ARM allowed the interest rate on the mortgage loan to be adjusted by 1 percent every six months (2 percent every year). These rate adjustments were tied to one of three indices: (1) the Federal Home Loan Bank Board's national mortgage rate closing index; (2) the three-year Treasury securities rate; or (3) the six-month Treasury bill rate. If rate changes (as calculated by the change in the index rate,) exceeded the "1 percent every six-month cap rule," the implied change could be carried over and used in the next adjustment period. There was no cumulative rate cap on the interest rate adjustment, though the six-month cap implied a 59 percent rate increase cap for a thirty-year mortgage. In terms of payment changes, the only restriction came indirectly—through the limitation on accumulated negative amortization. Negative amortization, which involves the adding of interest to the principal outstanding of the loan when monthly payments do not cover the interest payments due, was permitted under the ARM regulations as long as it is not in excess of 10 percent of the principal loan balance at the beginning of any five-year period. Thus, a very substantial interest rate rise could induce a payment increase to avoid violating the negative amortization rule. In March 1983 the comptroller of the currency regulations concerning the ARM were changed, in essence making them comparable to the AML regulations described below.

The adjustable mortgage loan (AML) regulations issued by the Federal Home Loan Bank were far more liberal. They provide virtually complete flexibility for the thrift institutions in designing various types of mortgage instruments. They set no ceiling on interest rate or payment adjustments, either annually or on a cumulative basis. They also have no restrictions on the cumulation of negative amortization, including negative amortization prior to the first rate adjustment (thus allowing the GPM-AML combination). The only requirement is that the index used for rate adjustment be readily verifiable by the borrower and not be under the control of the lender. Thus, any of the comptroller-suggested indices would be acceptable, as well as a wide range of market rates including the Federal Home Loan Bank cost-of-funds index. However, as of March 1983 all ARMs and AMLs made after that date face nearly identical, free market conditions.

The rationale behind allowing such a large amount of flexibility is that market competition will force both prudent and efficient limitations on the mortgage instrument. From the viewpoints of both lender and borrower, some form of payment cap seems essential. The lender wants to reduce the risk of default and thus should limit payment changes to some reasonable amount (e.g., 10 to 15 percent per year). The borrower also wants to limit payment changes so that they relate roughly to expected income changes. A popular alternative to the semi-annual payment adjustment mechanism appears to be the use of a fixed payment instrument for three to five years with a full payment adjustment at the third- or fifth-year mark (like a rollover mortgage, ROM). Any of these payment-capped (or fixed-payment) instruments might be subject to substantial negative amortization. Thus, lenders, secondary market purchasers, and private mortgage insurers should all limit the loan to current-market-value ratio to something less than 100 percent. In extremely unusual circumstances it is possible that the loan to current value ratio cap and the annual payment cap could come into conflict causing either a payment increase greater than 10 to 15 percent or a potential default on the property. We would consider this to be unlikely under most economic scenarios and under any reasonable set of initial pricing schemes.

While in general we feel that the market will adequately protect the consumer in terms of new mortgage instruments, there is a recent development that may require regulatory action. A number of savings and loans are marketing an AML with a substantially discounted interest rate. While this improves affordability it should be made clear to the consumer what rate is paid in year two, three, etc. if the index interest rate does not rise. There must be full and understandable disclosure to the consumer in all instances.

Graduated Payment Mortgage (GPM)

Since the essence of the borrower's problem is the upward shift in mortgage payments required in the early years of the mortgage loan due to the inflation premium in the interest rate, the obvious solution to this problem is a graduated payment mortgage (GPM). The GPM reduces payments in early years of the mortgage while allowing gradually increasing payments over time. Presumably, the increasing payments would be matched by increasing income due to the impact of inflation and real-wage growth on worker earnings. Thus, by taking advantage of the positive aspects of inflation's effect on income, there is a better match over time between mortgage loan payments and borrower's income. By alleviating the dynamic mismatch caused by the fixed payment-ixed interest rate mortgage, a good portion of the affordability crisis could be solved.

The GPM was first authorized for FHA mortgages in 1977 under the FHA-245 program. The Federal Housing Authority GPM sets limits on the amount of graduation and limits the period of graduated payments to ten years. The maximum graduation rate is 7.5 percent for five years or 3 percent for ten years. These provisions are highly restrictive and are in the process of being liberalized.

The GPM can also be issued on conventional mortgages, but as of this writing their use has not been widespread—primarily because of lower cash flow in early years and a perception of greater risk of default by the lender. On the other hand, all consumer surveys show borrowers strongly desire this type of loan.

It is our view that the widespread introduction of ARM, AML, and GPM mortgages and combinations of these mortgages will greatly enhance the options available to the consumer.

Chapter 5

Housing Policies for California in the 1980s

From our previous discussion it is clear that California faces a substantial set of housing problems in the mid-1980s. First time homebuyers and first entrants to the housing market will face a continuing affordability crisis, a function of the rise in house prices and interest rates in the 1970s. This first-time home-buyer affordability problem is having a substantial effect on the California economy by limiting its ability to attract and keep technical and professional employees. High housing costs are putting coastal metropolitan California at a substantial disadvantage in the competition for national economic growth. A set of policies that could reverse the relative rise in housing costs would clearly benefit both the California economy and young California families.

Despite the relative cost of California housing, California is likely to see strong demographic demand for housing for the remainder of the 1980s. Basic demand for housing units is over 230,000 per year for the next decade. The first three years of the decade, however, have seen housing production far below this basic demand level, implying that California may face a quantitative housing shortage when effective demand recovers.

The rental housing market, which experienced little new construction in the late 1970s and early 1980s, already is in the midst of a shortage condition. Rental vacancy rates in coastal metropolitan California are below 3 percent, considered far below the level necessary to provide for efficient and normal mobility in the housing market. In the last five years this has created pressure for rising rents and the corresponding political response of the introduction of rent control regulations. In addition to the quantitative shortage due to a lack of new construction, over 30 percent of Californians are paying more than 35 percent of their income for rental housing. Thus, the rental housing market faces both a shortage situation as well as an affordability crisis for certain low-income households.

The solution to California's housing problems are clearly complicated but revolve around one key fact—a high level of new production is needed in both the rental and homeownership sectors if present and future supply-demand imbalances and the corresponding further rise in relative prices are to be avoided. We now turn to an analysis of policies that move toward a solution to California's housing problems and the impact of these policies have on the state's economy.

ECONOMIC AND REVENUE IMPACT OF NEW HOUSING CONSTRUCTION

The direct economic impact of new housing production on the California economy can be quantified in a fairly accurate manner, using straightforward input-output and multiplier techniques. Table 1 shows our calculation of the output-, income- and employment-generating impacts per 100,000 California housing starts. We chose the measure of 100,000 starts because the spread between a "good" housing production year and a "bad" housing production year is roughly 100,000 units.

Table 1 shows that based on an average new home sales price*

---

*Use of "average" rather than "median" price is appropriate for an aggregate impact study.

Table 1. Impact of New Housing Construction on California Economy

	Dollars per Unit	Dollar Amount per 100,000 Units
Output generated		
Construction industry	69,143	$ 6.9 billion
Multiplier effect in other		
sectors	103,715	10.3 billion
Total	172,858	17.2 billion
Income generated		
Construction industry	22,817	2.2 billion
Other sectors	34,225	3.4 billion
Total	57,042	5.7 billion
Jobs created		
Construction	1.2	120,000
Other sectors	1.8	180,000
Total	3.0	300,000

of $128,500 and assuming from our earlier analysis that land costs comprise 35 percent of a new home, $83,525 in output is generated from each new home sale. Each apartment unit started is assumed to generate $47,571 in output, reflecting the smaller size of apartments and the lower proportion of land value to total value in apartment units. A weighted average of single family homes and apartments produces an average value of output per housing start of $69,143. Using a standard local multiplier effect of 1.5, meaning that each dollar of new housing production stimulates 1.5 dollars of output in other sectors, $103,715 of output per unit of housing is created in other sectors. Thus, the total output impact of a housing start is $172,858.

To translate the output generated into a measure of income generated we need to make an assumption concerning labor input and value added. Utilizing input-output analysis, about one-third of the value of housing construction represents value added. As a result, each unit started generates $22,817 in direct income and, using the 1.5 multiplier, generates $34,225 in indirect income for a total of $57,042 income per unit of housing started.

Employment created per housing unit is again dependent on the mix of housing units. A standard assumption is that about 1.2 man years per housing unit is required in direct employment and another 1.8 man years work is generated through the multiplier effect.

A translation of this new economic activity into tax revenue estimates is provided in Table 2. Three types of revenue are generally created from new housing construction: sales taxes, income taxes, and local property taxes. Assuming an effective average sales tax rate of 3 percent, when applied to our aggregate income number construction of a housing unit generates $1,711 in sales taxes. When applied to our aggregate income number, assuming an effective income tax rate of 5 percent produces $2,852 in income taxes per housing start. Using a 1 percent tax rate and applying it to the value of the housing starts plus land produces $864 per housing unit in local property taxes. In total, $5,427 in taxes are generated per housing start—$4,221 at the state level and $1,206 at the local level.

In addition to the direct economic and revenue impacts of new construction there is also a very important indirect benefit to the state of new housing production. Increased supply of housing in California could reduce the relative price disparity between California housing and the rest of the country. This in turn could produce more economic growth in California and induce more migration to the state. If the relative price of housing were reduced to only 20 percent over the national average (from 70 percent today), perhaps 1,000,000 more migrants would come to California in the next decade, increasing state GSP by $20 billion annually and increasing tax revenues by 1 billion annually. These people, however, would demand more state services, so it is not clear that economic growth due to migration is much of a net fiscal benefit to the state. It is clear, however, that a substantial additional amount of research work needs to be done on the relationship of housing costs to state economic and demographic growth. Except for our brief analysis of the relationship of housing costs to migration, it is beyond the scope of this study.

Table 2. Impact of New Housing Construction on California State and Local Tax Revenues

	Dollars per Unit	*Dollar Amount per 100,000 Units*
Income created	57,042	5.7 billion
Tax Revenues Anticipated		
Sales tax[a]	1,711	171 million
State	1,369	137 million
Local	342	34 million
State income tax[b]	2,852	285 million
Local Property Tax		
Increase in assessed value	86,428	8.6 billion
Property Tax Revenues		
(1 percent of value)	864	86 million
Total taxes	5,427	542 million
State	4,221	422 million
Local	1,206	121 million

[a]Assumed as an effective 3 percent rate.
[b]Assumed at an effective 5 percent rate.

ECONOMIC AND REVENUE IMPACT OF RESALE HOUSING TRANSACTIONS

The direct and indirect impacts of a resale transaction can be estimated in a fashion similar to the analysis for new construction. The income generated from the sale of an existing house can be calculated by looking at the direct expenditures of the household within a one-year period of the closing date of sale. Based on a median sale price of $113,000, the typical household spends about $1,400 prior to sale to fix up their housing unit. At the time of sale, various costs of closing including title insurance, escrow fees, termite and building inspection fees, appraisal and loan origination fees, and (of course) brokerage fees mean that each sale generates another $9,000 worth of service income. Following the purchase of a home, households typically make minor structural improvements and purchase furniture and appliances, generating an additional $4,000 in income. Thus total income for each existing home sale priced at $113,000 is roughly $14,400.

Table 3 documents these impacts per housing unit sold and per 100,000 units sold. As in the case of new housing construction, an income multiplier of 1.5 can be applied to the income generated from each home sale. The tax revenue calculations are then straightforward using the same rates as for the new construction case. The only major differences between the new construction estimates and the resale estimates relate to the increase in local property tax revenues. In the new construction case the entire value of the house goes into the property tax base, while in the resale case only the incremental value since 1975 goes into the base.

HOUSING POLICIES AND THE SUBSTITUTION EFFECT

The previous analysis documents the impact of housing activity, both new and existing, on state economic activity and on state and local tax revenues. It is not fair, however, to assume that state housing programs will have a one for one translation into economic- and revenue-producing activity. If the state funds a mortgage assistance program for 10,000 housing units, it will not mean that 10,000 additional housing units will be built or sold. This direct translation does not work because there is a substantial substitution effect between state programs and those units that the private sector would have sold or built anyway. This substitution effect might be small for a low income rental housing construction program, (i.e., not much would be built without the program) but might be large for a mortgage interest rate subsidy for middle-income homebuyers. This substitution effect is important when trying to calculate the net impact of state housing programs on the economy and the state's revenues. With this caveat in mind we now turn to an analysis of a set of programs to stimulate housing construction and sales in California.

Table 3. Impact of Resale Transaction on the California Economy and on State and Local Tax Revenues

	Dollars per Sale	*Dollar Amount per 100,000 Sales*
Income generated		
Pre-Sale Expenditures	1,400	140 million
Sale Expenditures		
Fees and Services	9,000	90 million
Post Sale Expenditures	4,000	400 million
Direct total income	14,400	1.44 billion
Multiplier effect in other sectors	21,600	2.16 billion
Total income	36,000	3.6 billion
Tax revenues anticipated		
Sales tax	1,080	108 million
State	864	86 million
Local	216	22 million
State income tax	1,800	180 million
Local property tax		
Increase in assessed value	33,900	33.9 billion
Property tax revenues	339	34 million
Total taxes	3,219	321 million
State	2,664	266 million
Local	555	55 million

PROPOSITION 5: CALIFORNIA FIRST-TIME HOMEBUYERS PLAN

In the fall of 1982 California voters passed Proposition 5, which authorized the issuance of up to $200 million in tax-exempt bonds to finance an interest rate buydown program for first-time homebuyers. In essence what Proposition 5 did was to provide the household with a temporary loan in the form of a second mortgage so that the household could construct a graduated-payment mortgage. The household would obtain a conventional loan from a financial institution with the Proposition 5 buydown provision attached. Thus, the households first year payments *and* qualifying criteria would be based on an interest rate in the 9 to 10 percent range because of the buydown. The difference between the market mortgage rate (13 to 14 percent) and the household's bought down rate would be paid out of the Proposition 5 bond proceeds or, if necessary, out of the state's general fund. The household's pay-ments would increase at a graduated rate of 5 percent a year, with the negative amortization in the early years continually paid by the state. As in the case of graduated payment, payments by the seventh year rise above those in the fixed payment case, and the negative amortization paid by the state begins to be paid off for the next seven years. At any time that the home is sold the negative amortization loan in paid off out of the proceeds of the sale.

The essence of the Cal-First program is that it attempts to encourage the use of a graduated-payment mortgage to increase first time homebuyer affordability. It attempts to greatly leverage the state's tax-exempt bond-issuing authority in the housing area by creating a shallow temporary subsidy to be fully repaid, rather a deep subsidy for thirty years, as is typical of the usual mortgage revenue bond. We calculate that temporary Proposition 5 subsidies would produce nearly seven times more housing per dollar than the usual MRB. Because of these features, the Cal-First program is far more cost efficient and could help more households than the conventional mortgage revenue bond proposals.

The comparative impact on the economy and on state and local tax revenues of $50 million in Cal-First Bonds and $50 million in conventional mortgage revenue bond financing is shown in Table 4.

The California First-Time Bonds would generate $373 million in output and nearly $201 million in additional net income in the state. State and local tax revenues would increase nearly $19 billion. These are clearly very high multiplier effects when com-pared to the much smaller effect of conventional mortgage revenue bonds. Thus, the Cal-First program is clearly a superior policy instrument.

Despite these positive policy features, as of early December 1983 the success of the Cal-First program was substantially in doubt. First, the failure of Congress to extend the authorization for tax-exempt mortgage revenue bonds means that the authori-zation for the issuance of such bonds will expire at year end. While there is a high liklihood that Congress will pass such an authorization in early 1984, the program will be temporarily sus-

Table 4. Impact of Cal-First Bonds and Conventional Mortgage Revenue Bonds on the California Economy and State and Local Tax Revenues

	Cal-First Bonds ($50 Million)	Conventional Mortgage Revenue Bonds ($50 Million)
Additional new housing units started[a]	2,156	313
Additional used housing units sold[a]	2,155	312
Output generated	373 million	54 million
Income created	201 million	29 million
Total taxes	18.6 million	2.7 million
State	14.8 million	2.5 million
Local	3.8 million	.55 million

[a]Assuming both bonds were divided equally among new and existing housing, average mortgage value of $80,000. Cal-First program assumes that a negative amortization subsidy with a present value of $11,603 is needed—a 4 percent buydown with a 5 percent per year graduated payment stream.

pended. Second, the response of lenders to the initial issue of the Cal-First Bonds has not been encouraging. Only $15 million of the $50 million available has been requested. There are probably a number of reasons for this poor response. First, most lenders are flush with money and would prefer to provide the borrowers adjustable rate mortgage loans at 10.5 to 11 percent. Second, the program is somewhat unusual, and the lenders may not be fully aware of potential consumer demand. Finally, since the Cal-First program is only a temporary shallow subsidy that must be repaid, it is less desirable to the potential borrower than the competing deep subsidy available from normal mortgage revenue bond programs.

To summarize, the Cal-First program is an extremely attractive policy instrument to improve first-time homebuyer affordability. A more active education and publicity campaign plus a curtailment of deep subsidy programs would make this program a viable state policy instrument.

YOUNG FAMILIES HOUSING ACT: A NEW INITIATIVE FOR FIRST-TIME HOMEBUYERS

The Cal-First program is a substantial step in the right direction in terms of improving affordability for first-time home-buyers. It takes advantage of two key affordability devices, tax-exempt mortgage revenue bonds and the graduated payment mortgage. It is only the later device, however, that matters, as the buyer eventually pays back the full amount of negative amortization in the Cal-First program.

In that case it seems that the goal of achieving affordability for the first-time entrant to the California housing market could more easily be achieved if the state were to set up a revolving fund to make all first-time homebuyers eligible for a temporary shallow-subsidy, graduated-payment loan. This fund could be raised through mortgage revenue bonds, general obligation bonds, or general revenue funds. The state would only fund the negative amortization portion of the loan with a payment by the state made on an annual basis to the private lender. Assuming a 4 percent negative amortization level in the initial year, 50,000 first-time homebuyers could be funded per year at a very modest up-front payment to the state—with of course all the money being paid back to the state with interest. Table 5 shows the time profile of revolving fund payments and the number of first-time homebuyers assisted. Clearly this sort of shallow subsidy approach, leveraging state money with private sector first mortgages is a potential solution to part of the affordability problem for first-time home-buyers.

REDUCING THE PRODUCTION COST OF HOUSING

While reducing the financing cost of housing for first-time buyers is of high priority, it is also critical to attempt to reverse the rise in relative house prices in California. Given our view that

Table 5. Young Families Housing Act Revolving Fund

	Households Assisted	State Payments for Negative Amortization
1984	50,000 @ 3200	160 million
1985	50,000 @ 2800	
	50,000 @ 3200	300 million
1986	50,000 @ 3200	
	50,000 @ 2800	
	50,000 @ 2400	420 million
1987	50,000 @ 3200	
	50,000 @ 2800	
	50,000 @ 2400	
	50,000 @ 2000	520 million
1988	Same Method	600 million
1989	Same Method	660 million
1990	Same Method	700 million

Note: From 1990 to 1996 the fund will decline as repayments begin; by 1996 repayments will offset new loans.

local land use regulations and the imposition of fees following the passage of Proposition 13 are the prime causes of the rise in relative prices, there are some clear actions that the state can take. The passage of AB2853 in 1980 mandated local governments to meet housing needs of the community and region. AB2853 not only mandates that communities accommodate housing but also specifies that they provide a mix of housing for all income groups. The implementation of these provisions is far more difficult than the idealistic passage of the legislation. A state-regional-local conflict has been set up that is in many cases difficult, if not impossible, to resolve. It appears that the only way to break this deadlock is for the state to allocate some "carrot" money. A simple proposal would be that communities allowing more housing activity in 1984 than in 1983 will be provided with, for example, a $1,500 fiscal impact grant for each unit in excess of 1983 production levels. In addition, local governments must regain the ability to pass advalorem bonds for meeting the infrastructure needs of new housing development. This would require a constitutional change in the Jarvis-Gann initiative. It is essential, however, to provide the communities with the financial resources to accommodate new growth.

Finally, it might be appropriate to attempt to simplify the environmental review process by eliminating judicial review of EIR's. Since the EIR process is advisory, there is no reason why the courts should have the ability to determine the adequacy of an EIR. The people are protected by the fact that local officials are elected and subject to recall. Furthermore, any action by local government is subject to the referendum. There is no reason to believe that judicial review of EIR's results in a better understanding of the environmental implications of a development.

RENTAL HOUSING INITIATIVE

The major problem faced by the rental housing market in California is a shortage of new production. There are four areas where policy changes might be made that could encourage more rental housing production: rent control regulation, local zoning regulations, the financing of rental units, and the taxation of rental units.

Rent Control Regulation

In order to bring stability to the rental housing industry, the state should adopt minimum standards for local residential rent controls. These standards should: (1) prohibit the regulation of rents on turnover; (2) permit a minimum annual prorated rent increase to tenants in place; and (3) Exempt new construction from rent control. While each of these measures is controversial, it is essential that the rent control issue be dealt with directly.

Local Zoning Regulation

A special land-use classification for rental housing (as opposed to condominium development) should be established to reduce the price of land and increase the supply of land for rental housing in coastal metropolitan California. Here perhaps the state could set some sort of minimum rental/owner zoning provision for vacant land. Also, the state might have higher "housing impact grants" for those communities that accept rental housing production.

Financing of Rental Units

Assuming that the state is again allowed to issue housing revenue bonds, a minimum proportion, (e.g., 40 percent) of this limited funding should be set aside for rental housing. A revolving loan fund to pay negative amortization cash flow on new rental housing could also be set up, with a graduate-payment mortgage being used on the rental property. As in the case of owner-occupied housing, this rental housing fund would be a shallow temporary subsidy that would be repaid by the borrower over the life of the loan or at resale. Finally, the state should develop a proposal that would encourage state pension funds to become equity partners in rental apartment construction to the same extent that they are partners in commercial construction.

Tax Law Change

The real estate syndication industry, which was founded in California, has in the past decade invested little new money in California rental housing. While the present rent control and threat of future rent control is largely to blame, it would seem appropriate to attempt to woo the syndication industry back to California. Perhaps California could pass an accelerated depreciation law that would allow new rental housing to be written off in say five years as compared with the longer IRS tax life of fifteen years. By making investing in new rental housing attractive, we could end the export of California money to the overbuilt Houston, Dallas, and Denver markets.

HOUSING FINANCE INITIATIVE

It is time for a review of the needs of the secondary mortgage market in the area of housing finance and the role to be played in it by the California Home Loan Mortgage Association (Callie Mae).

Callie Mae was authorized by legislation in 1982 but never implemented. It has the potential to fill the gap in capital needs that may result from inadequate levels of private and federal secondary market activity. It may, however, need a state loan for a successful start-up and may even require that the state put its "full faith and credit" behind Callie Mae's insurance guarantee for the first several years of operation. The importance of the secondary market is so vital to the California economy that it is clearly in the state's interest to activate Callie Mae.

In sum, the state of California is in a good position to initiate policies for first-time homebuyers, rental housing, and the secondary market that will insure adequate new construction and the production of affordable housing and adequate mortgage credit to meet the needs of a dynamic economy. Failure to meet the housing needs of its population could sharply curtail the economic growth of California in the mid- and late-1980s.

Appendix

While this book primarily deals with an aggregate analysis of the California housing market in the 1980s, we have in this Appendix attempted to set out some of the very substantial differences in demand, affordability, and supply which are occurring in the different metropolitan areas. While it is of necessity a cursory and numerical treatment of California's diversity it will hopefully provide some additional insights into the California housing market.

Table A.1   Total Population (Thousands)

	1960	1970	1980	1990E
California	15870	20333	23096	27696
SMSA				
Anaheim		1484	1892	2301
Bakersfield	292	336	393	517
Fresno	366	425	506	385
Los Angeles	6743	7104	7401	7899
Modesto		200	261	340
Oxnard		396	512	654
Riverside	810	1171	1497	2261
Sacramento	503	830	991	1249
Salinas		253	287	354
San Diego	1033	1392	1828	2276
San Francisco	2783	3119	3226	3433
San Jose	642	1101	1271	1467
Santa Barbara	169	270	295	322
Santa Cruz		130	184	225
Santa Rosa		212	292	365
Stockton	250	296	338	445
Vallejo		260	323	421

E = Estimate

Source: U.S. Bureau of the Census and RDA/Chase Econometrics

Table A.2   Population Growth (Thousands)

| | 1970-1980 | | 1980-1990 | |
	Increase	% Inc.	Increase	% Inc.
California	2763	13.6	4599	19.9
SMSA				
Anaheim	408	27.5	409	21.6
Bakersfield	57	17.0	124	31.5
Fresno	82	19.2	79	15.6
Los Angeles	297	4.2	498	6.7
Modesto	61	30.6	79	30.4
Oxnard	116	29.4	142	27.7
Riverside	326	27.8	764	51.0
Sacramento	161	19.4	258	26.0
Salinas	34	13.5	67	23.4
San Diego	435	13.3	449	24.6
San Francisco	107	3.4	207	6.4
San Jose	171	15.5	196	15.4
Santa Barbara	25	9.4	27	9.1
Santa Cruz	54	41.6	41	22.3
Santa Rosa	79	37.4	74	25.2
Stockton	42	14.2	106	31.5
Vallejo	63	24.2	98	30.4

Table A.3 Estimated Number of Households (Thousands)

	1980 Households	1990 Estimated Households
California	8629.9	10046.8
SMSA		
Anaheim	686.3	813.4
Bakersfield	138.5	176.2
Fresno	178.5	202.1
Los Angeles	2730.5	2878.8
Modesto	94.7	120.0
Oxnard	172.8	211.4
Riverside	551.6	792.7
Sacramento	383.8	469.9
Salinas	95.7	116.3
San Diego	670.1	814.5
San Francisco	1280.5	1350.2
San Jose	458.5	517.9
Santa Barbara	109.3	117.8
Santa Cruz	71.8	85.1
Santa Rosa	114.5	138.5
Stockton	124.6	158.8
Vallejo	117.1	146.2

Source: U.S. Bureau of the Census and Chase Econometrics/RDA.

Table A.4 Median Sales Price of Existing Homes

	May 1980	May 1982	May 1983
California	98,994	110,236	113,896
Region			
Los Angeles	103,884	118,845	111,382
San Francisco	106,783	120,310	126,841
San Diego	79,472	99,802	102,682
Orange County	108,315	137,791	134,237
Central Valley	61,797	72,215	71,140
Palm Springs	126,315	85,832	89,443
Monterey	99,704	109,499	109,399
Northern California	59,713	62,666	58,808
Riverside	68,116	80,749	79,068
Ventura	102,571	NA	137,107

Source: California Association of Realtors

Table A.5   California Housing Permits

	1970	1971	1972	1973	1974	1975	1976
California	194.8	255.2	279.3	216.3	127.3	130.7	219.7
SMSA							
Anaheim	23.4	31.2	35.8	28.2	17.8	15.4	30.2
Bakersfield	2.6	2.4	3.6	2.3	2.2	2.6	4.4
Fresno	4.7	6.2	6.8	4.8	4.2	4.3	6.8
Los Angeles	46.8	44.8	52.9	42.9	20.1	17.7	29.3
Modesto	2.0	3.1	3.6	2.8	2.2	2.2	3.9
Oxnard	5.3	8.1	7.4	5.6	2.7	5.0	8.5
Riverside	9.9	15.2	19.8	15.5	8.0	10.5	19.8
Sacramento	11.6	14.2	16.7	12.8	8.8	10.0	5.7
Salinas	1.7	3.0	3.9	2.7	1.6	2.1	2.9
San Diego	22.7	36.5	38.3	24.6	14.9	13.3	29.1
San Francisco	25.4	38.8	36.1	27.2	12.0	12.1	16.8
San Jose	17.8	19.6	14.9	12.9	9.0	8.2	13.2
Santa Barbara	1.8	2.1	3.4	3.6	1.6	1.3	1.9
Santa Cruz	1.8	2.8	3.7	2.3	1.1	1.3	2.3
Santa Rosa	2.7	4.4	5.3	4.0	3.7	2.8	3.8
Stockton	2.7	3.2	3.6	2.9	3.0	2.7	4.4
Vallejo	3.3	4.3	4.1	4.4	1.5	3.1	4.0

Table A.5 California Housing Permits

	1977	1978	1979	1980	1981	1982	Jan to Oct 1983
California	270.9	245.3	211.5	144.4	104.2	85.0	139.7
SMSA							
Anaheim	27.5	19.2	17.6	10.9	9.4	5.4	10.4
Bakersfield	5.1	4.9	4.8	3.0	2.6	4.4	5.1
Fresno	6.3	7.3	5.3	3.8	2.2	1.8	5.0
Los Angeles	39.3	40.3	36.6	28.8	21.1	14.4	19.2
Modesto	5.2	4.1	3.2	2.3	1.2	1.0	1.5
Oxnard	8.5	8.3	5.9	4.0	2.8	1.1	2.8
Riverside	34.7	33.1	28.0	16.2	12.9	10.8	20.1
Sacramento	20.1	15.9	17.6	9.6	5.9	5.6	9.3
Salinas	2.3	2.5	1.9	1.2	0.9	0.7	0.9
San Diego	36.4	28.3	19.2	13.2	9.0	7.5	17.7
San Francisco	21.9	20.1	18.2	14.2	9.7	8.9	12.7
San Jose	12.9	10.5	8.1	7.9	3.7	2.9	4.7
Santa Barbara	2.5	2.1	2.3	1.5	1.4	1.1	1.6
Santa Cruz	2.7	2.5	1.6	1.4	1.3	1.1	0.9
Santa Rosa	4.9	3.6	4.1	2.5	1.4	1.6	3.2
Stockton	5.5	6.3	4.9	2.4	2.0	2.4	3.2
Vallejo	6.5	5.3	3.9	2.6	1.7	2.0	2.9

Source: RDA/Chase Econometrics